We
the "Dismukeses"

I honor You —
to You Transformation

Rom 12:1-2

21
Ts to
TRANSFORMATION

How Do I Move From Here To There?

GENE C. BURGESS

21 TS TO TRANSFORMATION HOW DO I MOVE FROM HERE TO THERE? BY GENE C. BURGESS

Published by: TSH PUB
ISBN: 978-0-9911034-0-9
Copyright © 2013 by Gene Burgess
Cover design by: Ken Raney and Image Plus

Available in print from your local bookstore, online, or from the author at: Sales@21-TS.COM. Quantity discounts also available at Sales@21-Ts.com.

For more information on this book and the author: www.GeneBurgess.com.

Library of Congress Cataloging-in-Publication Data
Burgess, Gene C.
21 Ts to Transformation How do I move from here to there? / Gene C. Burgess, 1st ed.

Printed in the United States of America.

CONTENTS

DEDICATED TO

ZIG ZIGLAR
(and all good teachers)

Zig Ziglar passed to another world, November 28, 2012.

In 1996 my son Tucker and I read one page of Ziglar's
Over the Top
to several teenage boys in an orphanage in Haiti.

I wrote Mr. Ziglar, thanking him for making the truths in his book just as relevant to children abandoned in the streets of Haiti as people who make a million dollars a year.

To Zig and all teachers who make their messages simple, true, and full of love.

This book is dedicated to you!

We need more of your kind.

GUARANTEE

This publication contains the ideas of its author (and several dozen other people). This book intends to provide helpful ideas on the subject addressed—Transforming Ideas into Reality. The principles outlined may not be suitable for everyone and are not guaranteed or promised to produce any particular result or take you to any particular destination. The results are up to you.

The ideas offered here have worked for the author to move him to his desired *there*.

The Ts have not been completed. The author is certain that more ideas (Ts) are available which could be added to this formula. Search for them as you read. As you find those insights, please forward them to us at: Submissions@21-Ts.com. We want to learn as we Teach.

If you find *21 Ts* unworkable in your life, we will gladly refund 100% of the purchase price. Return the book with the receipt (address posted at 21-Ts.com) and we will return your money, no questions asked.

PROLOGUE

A school administrator asked several sign companies to develop concepts for wall graphics for an elementary school. The *best* idea(s) would be permanently displayed to motivate the students.

Our goal: to find that idea.

We wondered:

- What it would take to captivate teachers with the entire process of education and the Transformation of students?
- What would be required to Transform a five-year-old, who cannot read twenty-one words, into a ten-year-old, who reads twenty-one thousand?

As we uncovered principles required to Transform Ideas into Reality, we created short phrases and images to display those concepts graphically. To verify that the phrases and images were true, we compiled a story for each principle. The principles shared in *21 Ts* evolved from that research.

The great news is, it does not matter where our *here* is or where our desired *there* is. The steps to *there* always start *here*.

How do we move from *here* to *there*? *21 Ts* will help you identify the principles required to make the Transition to Transformation. Let's start adding Ts.

T + here = There

INTRODUCTION

Ben was born in the inner city of Detroit. His mother only finished the third grade and she married at thirteen. Ben's parents divorced when he was eight, which required his mother to work many jobs to provide for her two sons. But she still found a way to invest in her boys. She limited them to two television programs a week. To invest their energy more wisely, she had them read two books a week and then give her reports. Within a year, Ben went from an angry, troubled boy to a young man who amazed his teachers and fellow students. Ben Carson went on to become an incredible surgeon and the Chief of Staff at John Hopkins Medical University.

Nido Qubein expresses a transformational principle in his book, *Seven Choices for Success and Significance*, in which he says, "Your present circumstances don't determine where you can go; they merely determine where you start."

How do you plan to move from *here* to *there*? If you don't like your *here* and want to go *there*, your inability to reach your *there* can make your *here* . . . seem undesirable. But if you make a decision to leave *here*, what will you need to reach your dream? Who will help you in the Transition from *here* to *there*?

Steve Harrison promoted a seminar with Jack Canfield like this: "When he was first starting out, Jack Canfield had almost completely maxed out his credit cards and 144 publishers had rejected his book, ***Chicken Soup for the Soul***. But he never gave up on his dream of being a best-selling author. Today Jack is arguably the most successful, best-selling, non-fiction author of all time. He has over 500 million books in print and has launched forty-seven *New York Times* best-sellers (and even had seven books simultaneously on the list at one point). How did Jack get from where he was to where he really wanted to be?"

Mr. Harrison is right. No one will argue that Mr. Canfield's idea is worthy of consideration. 144 publishers, regrettably, might not have thought so, but that does not change the fact that 500 million other people did. How did Mr. Canfield go from *here* (an inner-city school teacher) to *there* ("the most successful, best-selling non-fiction author of all time")? How did he maneuver that Transformation? What was his formula?

You may find yourself where Ben or Jack found themselves. *here,* desiring to go *there.* Don't let your current circumstances stop you from achieving your goal. You, just like Ben and Jack, can step into a process of Transformation.

What is the difference in the words each and teach? Title and tile? Or here and there? By definition, there are great differences. Looking at the letters—in all three illustrations—it is just a T.

This book offers twenty-one Ts that can have as dramatic an impact on your life as adding a T at the beginning of the word here.

I need a *Teacher* to help me
move from here to there . . .

CHAPTER A

Teacher

A gentle wind blows across the Denny's parking lot. The cool breeze sweeps fallen leaves to the curb, and I zip my coat to protect myself from the chill. Sometimes, in an unplanned moment like this, the ordinary can become Transformational.

As I chat with three other businessmen, I realize they are nothing like me. They are from varied educational, social, and financial backgrounds. Paul makes in excess of one million dollars a year. The others earn $400,000, $100,000 and $15,000. (I'm the $15.)

As we prepare to leave, Paul asks me, "What language do you speak?"

"English," I say without thought. *What a lame question for such a well-informed man.*

"How did you learn English?" Paul asks.

"My family speaks English. I grew up around it."

Then Paul asks what seems to be another unnecessary question. "What type of foods do you eat?"

"Chicken . . . roast beef . . . potatoes . . . grits and eggs. The normal stuff."

"How did you learn to enjoy those foods?"

I don't understand the purpose of this pop quiz, but answer nonetheless.

"Again, I would have to say, I grew up around it."

Paul is not distracted by cars pulling in and out of the parking lot. His complete focus is on me. Our eyes lock as he asks *the* question: "How do you make a million dollars a year?"

"I wish I knew," I respond with a chuckle.

Paul smiles. "But you do know. You just told me twice."

"Come on . . . learning English and eating chicken have nothing to do with making money."

Paul looks over his glasses, again locking eyes with mine. "I understood you to say you associated with people who speak English and eat chicken . . . then with little to no effort, you said you learned their vocabulary and to enjoy their foods?"

"Yeah, but . . ."

As I struggled for the words, Paul gently asked, "Correct?"

"Yes," I respond, as my face turns red. We are almost detached from the other men. Paul and I are suspended in a moment as he continues with the skill and precision of a brain surgeon.

"If you were to associate with people who make a million dollars a year, do you think you could learn to make more money, just like you learned English?"

The chilling breeze stops. In the stillness of the moment, the leaves lay still beside the curb. I am calm, almost warm. We have nothing more to say, so we depart for our respective homes.

A Glance Back to Focus the Future

Paul gave me direction for my future—by pointing to my past. That cool fall evening found me between jobs. I was unemployed, with a wife and three sons. Prior to that, I accepted a job designed to last one year. The job allowed us an opportunity to live on Antigua in the Caribbean. But the year ended and I was back in the States looking for direction, another job, and cash. I was looking for another job until that encounter with Paul. After that conversation, I quit looking for a job and started looking for a *Teacher*.

Since birth, my family, associations, and the books I read influenced my destiny. For the most part, that influence came without my consent. I never planned to speak English. I was just present as the attitudes, behavior, and communication (a-b-c) patterns of my Teachers were becoming mine. When people spoke, used an electric food blender, or hit their finger with a hammer, I was being Transformed. In every way I was, without a doubt, *becoming like* my Teachers.

How to Start Moving from Here to There

As I reflect on that evening, I realize I was in that parking lot because of a simple invitation from a business colleague. "Would you like to meet my friend Paul?" It was *just* a twenty-one-second phone conversation that *just* happened to Transform my destiny. Sometimes my Teachers were there day after day, like my parents. Other times they came through an invitation like this one. Almost without consent, Transformation was taking place on a regular basis.

Paul showed me that if I wanted to be Transformed into a plumber, all I had to do was spend Time with plumbers, read books about plumbing, master the use of plumbing Terms and Tools, and soon I would be a plumber. It would happen as you would expect, if I remained under the Teacher's influence.

From that moment, I was determined to select my Teachers and those I allowed to influence my life, with care. The books I would read, the people I would associate with, and the TV personalities I permitted to enter my air space were taking me somewhere. They were going to potentially determine the new language I would speak (Chapter G Training). Meeting an unknown receptionist and having a forty-five second discussion about a career track might change my future (Chapter L Trade). Even if it was *just* a twenty-one-second phone call or a thirty-second radio ad, I was going to consider the potential consequences. A brief conversation could influence where my energy, Time, and money would go for years. I needed to be active in choosing my Teachers (Chapter U Test 1).

John Wooden, basketball coach and mentor repeated this poem in a speech he delivered:

No written word no spoken plea
Can teach our youth what they should be

> Not all the books on all the shelves
> But what the Teachers are themselves.
> (Author unknown)

Phil Driscoll, a world-class trumpet player/composer and a Grammy award-winning performer, understands the power of a Teacher. His son told him he wanted to learn to play the trumpet. Phil told him, "You were born into the right family."

Does this principle apply to everything—learning a language, enjoying a career, or certain foods? Even developing a new business? Can traits we pick up along the way be attributed to being around a good, or not-so-good, Teacher? Finding the right Teacher is a key to being Transformed into whatever we want to become. Please allow me to repeat myself. After that conversation with Paul, I quit looking for a job and started looking for a Teacher. So I leave you with two questions:

- Where do you want to go?
- Who has the experience to show you how to get there?

A SIMPLE OBSERVATION:
> Moving from *here* to *there*, wherever *there*
> might be—requires a Teacher.

THINGS TO THINK THROUGH:
- From this moment, how will you choose your Teachers?
- Who will you allow to Teach (influence) you?
- Will their knowledge and skill-set lead you to where you want to go?
- How will you guard your mind so you don't absorb a-b-c traits you do not desire?
- My friend Daniel Ross says, "You don't get what you deserve, but what you pursue." What Teachers and mentors are you pursuing?

ANCIENT WRITINGS: "Sir," he said, "we all know that God has sent you to teach us."

BOOK: *The Greatest Salesman in the World* by Og Mandino

I WILL APPLY THIS PRINCIPLE BY:_____

_____

_____

_____

I need a Teacher to help me
move from here to there. When
I have a *Target* . . .

CHAPTER B

Target

Danny Lemmons was a picture of perfection. He had the looks, build, and personality to become a champion. But Danny lacked determination, focus, and a Target. At that Time, Danny was going through life, only concerned about eating, sleeping, and . . . girls. He was neglecting the disciplines of success. That was until he focused on winning a state championship ring in wrestling. According to Mary Kay Ash, owner of Mary Kay cosmetics, "Ideas are a dime a dozen, people who implement them are priceless." Flirting with an idea and pursuing one are two *entirely* different things.

Danny began to seek guidance about every decision from his coaches. He embraced their suggestions regarding his diet, workout routines, and commitment to academics. Tony Miller, who authored *Journey to Significance,* said, "Everyone wants to be prosperous. But few develop the disciplines required to be prosperous." Danny not only followed his coach's instructions, he enjoyed implementing prosperous habits. He became enthusiastic about the new process.

Unfortunately, a torn meniscus brought Danny's season to a halt; nevertheless his Target still drives him to train. To win that ring he cannot be nonchalant about recuperating. He has to remain in tune with his coaches and follow their instructions.

21 Ts To Transformation   GENE C. BURGESS

Embracing Transformation

David Culpepper came into James Alverson's high school algebra class grumbling, "Why do I need to learn this?"

Mr. Alverson responded, "David, are you asking, 'Why is this important?'"

"Yeah, this stuff has no use."

Trying to relieve the tension, Mr. Alverson asked, "David, what is your goal in life?"

David softened and responded, "I want to own a restaurant."

"Owning a restaurant is a worthy Target. There are many subjects you will need to master, but let's focus on algebra."

"Okay, why do I need to learn algebra?"

"Who will pay the bills at your new restaurant?"

"I will," David responded with a note of arrogance.

"Technically that is true," Mr. Alverson added, smiling, "but could we say, since you do not have an endless supply of cash, your customers will pay the bills?"

David agreed, slightly embarrassed.

"Would you agree every business hopes to have income?"

"Yep," David said pleasantly.

"Let's call income—intake. Along with intake, every business has a variety of expenses which we will call outflow." Mr. Alverson wrote those words on the board.

"As a class," Mr. Alverson continued, "let's list everything that would be considered intake and outflow."

The students began to propose items to list on the intake and outflow sides of the equation. Some were known, such as the rent and insurance. Others suggested materials used and utilities. Then someone offered variables dependent on quantity, storage and wages. Finally, someone suggested the owner must make a profit.

Mr. Alverson wrote an *F* on the board. "David, the owner has to calculate all *fixed* overhead costs. Next, you will estimate the number of *customers* you hope to serve." He then placed a *C* on the board.

"What are other variables you have to know as a restaurateur?"

26

"A pancake will sell for less than a steak," David answered.

"Correct. Income will vary depending on the foods the customers buy, as well as the number of meals served. So we have two new variables. The $ will represent price and *I* will represent the potential income."

Mr. Alverson proceeded. "You will buy pancake mix for less than steaks. *G* will represent cost of goods. Finally, the other expenses must be included." He wrote on the board: *P* is for desired profit, *R* for return on investment, *T* for taxes, *E* for employee expenses.

"David, if you do not know these variables, you can lose money. Guess who will pay the bills then?" Mr. Alverson asked with a smile.

"I will." The class joined in the laughter.

"Therefore, the answer to, 'Why do I need to learn algebra?' is simple. Without knowledge, you could fail."

The class looked at the equation. F/C + $/I + G + (P+R+T+E) = Price per Item / Potential Success.

"Today, rather than turning to page 138, we will consider what David will have to know—and do—to stay in business."

Mr. Alverson recalls David enjoying algebra with a passion after that conversation. When you have a Target, your coach or Teacher's value increases greatly. Additionally, you will begin discovering the treasures buried within you.

Your Target and This Book

The purpose of this book is not to tell you which Target to select or which Teachers to pursue. This book *is* designed to encourage you to find a Target that ignites your passions and inspires you to action. Once you have that Target in mind, you will need to pursue the right Teacher(s).

Many people, however, had valuable ideas that were wasted. The foundation required to support that dream was never built and the idea collapsed. This book outlines a process of building that foundation.

You may have many ideas. Dr. Seuss wrote (in *Oh, the Places You'll Go!*), "You have the brains in your head. You have the feet in your shoes. You can steer yourself any direction you choose." Since you cannot pursue every dream, which one will you pursue?

Consider Mr. Arthur J. Hoist's poem, *Goal*.

As I paused to *think* of something, that sets some men apart,
it seems to me that goals in life, must be the place to start.
Imagine playing football, on an unmarked field of green,
not a goal line to be sought, not a goal post to be seen.
It would be an aimless battle, were there nothing to be gained.
Without a thing to strive for, not a score to be attained.
We must have purpose in our life, for the flame that warms the
soul is an everlasting vision, every man must have his goal.

If your desired Target does not empower you with possibilities, passion, and purpose now—dream bigger. Gilbert Kaplan, journalist, professor and investor said, "When everybody tells you that you are being idealistic or impractical, consider the possibility that everybody could be wrong about what is right for you." Someone more than likely laughed at Kaplan's dream, but he sold that dream (Institutional Investor magazine), for seventy-two million dollars ($72,000,000). Where will your dream take you?

Choosing Your Target

You might feel you have little to no hope of moving from *here* to (your desired) *there*. When you find that Target, which moves your emotions, will, mind, soul, and body, you are about to launch yourself into a totally new world. Your destiny does not have to live in custody to past failures and experiences. You can break free and be catapulted by a new idea.

Mr. Earl Nightingale, a motivational speaker and author said, "People with goals (*Targets*) succeed because they know where they're going (emphasis mine)." They also understand mentors are needed to guide them.

Dr. John Maxwell, leadership expert, gave a speech on success. I paraphrase but he said, "There are two important days in your life. The day you were born and the day you figure out why."

A SIMPLE OBSERVATION:

Moving from *here* to *there*, wherever *there* might be—requires a
Target and a Teacher
(and action . . . or you could end up right *here*).

THINGS TO THINK THROUGH:

- Where do you want to go?
- Do you have a Target?
- Is the Teacher able to give you the correct guidance?
- What is right/wrong with your current *here*? Why?
- Is your current *here* filled with passion about your desired *there*? If not, have you picked the right Target?

ANCIENT WRITINGS: "Where there is no revelation, people cast off restraint; but blessed is the one who heeds wisdom's instruction."

BOOK: *Creating Your Own Destiny* by Patrick Snow

I WILL APPLY THIS PRINCIPLE BY:_____

_____

_____

_____

I need a Teacher to help me move from here to there. When I have a Target, the proper Teacher will naturally *Transmit* . . .

CHAPTER C

Transmit

Mike Seczawa, my great-nephew-in-law, lives near the St. Clair River in Michigan. One day he helped me repair a pressure tank for a well. As Mike worked, I watched in amazement at his proficiency. I wanted to know what he knew and how he learned it, so I asked him about his work, skills, and history.

From as early as six, he said he disassembled the electronic toys he received as Christmas presents and reworked the mechanisms. He recalled his father asking him to rework an electric socket at age seven. But when Mike was eleven he built a friendship with an older man named Hank. Hank was *just* a neighbor, but he became a mentor. As Mike began to tell me about Hank, tears started streaming down his face.

Hank and Mike decided to build an ice shanty for fishing. That is not an unusual task for neighbors to cooperate on, living on the St. Clair River. When the ice thickened, they dragged the shanty from the brush to the center of the river.

"We need a snowmobile," Mike said to Hank.

"Those things are a little expensive to pull a shanty to its proper location twice a year," Hank said. Nevertheless, he agreed and started looking for one.

When he found a used one, Hank told Mike, "I will show you how to rebuild it. If you will do the work, this snowmobile will be yours when we are finished."

"Hank explained the process, every step of the way," Mike said. "We located the broken part in a scrap yard and had a new machine in no time."

They may have Transformed the machine, but the bigger Transformation occurred in Mike. The tears that streamed down Mike's face were not the result of a man fixing a snowmobile. Instead, they were the result of Hank Transmitting his heart to Mike.

Mike loves installing expensive gadgets on million-dollar yachts. That is what Mike does Today as his chosen Trade.

A Process for Transmitting Knowledge

Dr. Keith Drury is a college professor and the author of: *Money, Sex & Spiritual Power*, and *So, What Do You Think?* He explains the Transmission process with a word picture: Ah-choo.

Dr. Drury might explain this principle with an illustration such as: "I have the flu; but I describe to you how you will feel if you get the measles. No matter how much you learn about the measles, when we part, what will I Transmit to you?"

When mentors Transmit information, it is the equivalent of "sneezing" on you. People live and die because of Transmissions. The verb "Transmit" means to send something, pass something on, or cause something to spread, from one person, thing, or place, to another. According to Dr. Drury, three truths must exist in order for the Ah-Choo to be effective.

1. The Teacher must be infected.
2. Time is required for the infection to set in.
3. The student cannot be immune.

The Teacher Must Be Infected

When you select a Teacher, you need to make sure he *has* what you need. If you decide swimming is your goal, the principles your mentor shares must be something he *breathes*. Rather than trying to convince you how much he loves to swim, he should take you to a pool and jump in with you. When you experience his love and passion for swimming, it will be contagious. More is caught than taught in the Transmission process. Education should be natural, like learning to speak or eat at the family table.

In *The Millionaire Messenger*, Brendon Burchard describes meeting Tony Robbins this way: "It was not just what he was saying; it was what he was *displaying*."

In the 1980s, a school board asked a committee to review and recommend a sex education curriculum for our district. As a member of that board, I made an observation. "To me it does not seem to be important what curriculum we use. If we have a Teacher who thinks teens are going to be sexually active and that a condom is the best solution, no matter how much abstinence curriculum we select, the students will *get* what their Teacher *thinks*. The curriculum will not be the deciding factor. The Teacher will. The real question should be: Who is going to Teach the students?"

Curriculum is important and should be accurate, but the Teacher is more important. If the Teacher says, "Practice safe sex, abstain," but has a smirk on his face and a wink in his eye, his students will easily be infected with the real message. When someone speaks, they Transmit concepts, attitudes, and spirit beyond the words themselves. When we select our Teachers, we need to understand that they will Transmit who they really are.

My friend, Luis Rodriguez, described his mentor this way: "His leadership abilities flow from him like sweat when you work." That is the kind of infectious influence our Teachers need to have. When they infect us with information (hopefully, Truth-Chapter M), it should occur without effort.

Time is Required

Dr. Drury shares that when we decide to let someone ah-choo on us, we need to spend enough Time with the Teacher to absorb the infection. Time is essential for permanent Transformation. The more Time we can spend with our Teachers, the better chance we have of being infected with whatever they have. That is why choosing our Teachers is so important (more on this in Chapters G Training and O Time).

Kristy Tipton, a friend and neighbor in the 80s, handed me a German grammar book. Opening the first page, I read, "Millions of people study languages they never learn and millions of people learn languages they never study." We will not remember terms without continuous exposure to them. However, with Time and repeated exposure, the natural process of Transformation will take place—with or without our consent. We don't set out to get the flu. It just happens if we are exposed. Transmissions of attitudes, behaviors, and communication skills (a-b-c) are inevitable with Time and exposure (unless a person is immune—which we will discuss).

How many have studied the "German language" for three years and cannot remember three words? How many children have never studied German, but by being immersed in it can speak thousands of words? Find Teachers who can Transmit over Time.

Make Sure You Are Not Immune

"When possible," Dr. Drury explains, "make sure the student is not immune." If your mentor endeavors to Transmit something to you and you have no natural gifting or interest (or even temperament), you will find the process much more burdensome for both you and the Teacher.

If you try to Teach me anything about mechanics, you will not have much success. I know what a wrench is and how it works, but the last Time I changed the oil in my car (1991) it took me five hours on a beautiful Saturday. This is why I love my mechanic.

While visiting in Antigua, I saw a former neighbor I had not seen in twenty years. I called to her over the fence, but she didn't acknowledge me. So, I repeated myself several times, but she never turned around. Later that afternoon I saw her brother and we chatted on the concrete porch in the Caribbean breeze. He said, "She is deaf." I could not Transmit my greetings by way of speech because of the hearing loss.

We can waste a lot of our Teacher's Time and precious energy if our hearts and heads are not in tune with the subject. Gilbert K. Chesterton says, "Education is simply the soul of a society as it passes from one generation to another." If you are not open to learning the wisdom of those who have gone before, the effort can be painful.

Do you remember required classes in high school and college? With the future I had planned, I could not understand how chemistry could help me. Actually, the thought of having to study the subject—which gave me no hope of a future identity or possible income—turned me off.

Until we become engaged and excited about the benefits of knowing or receiving whatever is being Transmitted, our immune system is working overtime to protect us from being infected. A good Teacher (Chapter A) who knows he must Transmit the required material, should consider spending class time explaining other applications or reasons to study the required material. Having a Target can weaken our immune system and open our minds.

I was out of college before I learned these principles. Dr. Drury was right. I was naturally absorbing much more from the professors than the words and equations they taught. I was becoming *like* them. My friend and missionary Daniel Ross says, "We teach what we know. But we reproduce what we are."

What are your mentors reproducing in you?

A SIMPLE OBSERVATION:
Transmissions work naturally—for the good germs and bad!
Be careful, someone is sneezing.
Sometimes it's you—what are you spreading?

THINGS TO THINK THROUGH:
- Who has *infected* you?
- Was it with or without your consent? Why?
- Did it happen naturally?
- What process did the Teacher use?
- Who needs to infect you now? Why?

ANCIENT WRITINGS: "Let the wise listen and add to their learning, and let the discerning get guidance."

BOOK: Any book about Mother Teresa. She Transmitted who she was to the world.

I WILL APPLY THIS PRINCIPLE BY: _____

_____

_____

_____

I need a Teacher to help me move from here to there. When I have a Target, the proper Teacher will naturally Transmit the *Terms* . . .

CHAPTER D

Terms

Marckens and Alejandro are both twelve years old. Both have loving parents and are healthy, but they are headed in different directions.

Marckens was born in Haiti, Alejandro in Costa Rica. Marckens will have about a 60% chance to learn to read whereas Alejandro a 99% likelihood. Marckens has a 21% chance of reaching secondary school, Alejandro 95%. In Haiti, 55% of the people live on less than $1.25 a day. In Costa Rica, only 1% of the people live at that low of an income. If Marckens lives in a rural area, his chances of having proper sanitation and running water are about 10%. In comparison, Alejandro a 90% likelihood.

Statistics can be inaccurate and people do overcome the odds, but they also convey general truths. Why are Marckens and Alejandro facing completely different futures? Why such diverse opportunities?

Let's consider other barriers and opportunities we face, before we answer those questions. What are our chances of learning to be a brain surgeon if we don't know what a medulla oblongata is? Or an electrician if we don't know what an amp or ohm is? How could we cook or order a meal if we don't understand the Terms in the cookbook or menu?

Learning the Terms

When an individual dreams of becoming a doctor, electrician, or chef, he or she will start with the Terms. As a person begins to study those sciences, many of the Terms will seem foreign. My introduction to writing came from my editor, Lee Warren. In my first official discussion with Lee, he handed me a *Glossary of Terms for Publishing*. The Terms were a *new language* and a new foundation, which Lee knew I needed.

Kathy Willis led a Teacher training seminar. As she drew several circles and random lines on the board, she said, "Every letter originally looked like *that* to you—a mess. Over Time, what were originally unrecognizable shapes took on sounds and, eventually, meaning. Thus you mastered the alphabet." She encouraged us to remember that without the foundational knowledge of the Terms we use, our students will not understand.

These next symbols, which are actual Terms (words), may look like a mess to you also: 神 愛 世 人 ， 甚 至 將 他 的 獨 生 子 賜 給 他 們 ， 叫 一 切 信 他 的 ， 不 至 滅 亡 ， 反 得 永 生. This will only become plain to our eye and mind when we master the sound and meaning of each Chinese character and what it means in relation to the next.

Teresa Wilson, a friend, handed me the menu from Uncle Poon's Chinese Restaurant. I read, "Szechuan, Subgum, Wonton, and Moo Goo Gai Pan." Even when the characters find their English equivalent, without understanding the Terms and their definition, we do not know which meal we desire. The same principle applies to our dream. We need a new set of Terms—Terms we recognize and understand—if we are going to move towards and function in a new Trade or specialty.

Terms Determine the Difference

I thought I had ordered an 18" graphic from a supplier for my sign company. Upon arrival, I started unrolling and unrolling and unrolling the graphic . . . way beyond 18". I called the manufacturer. "Why did you send me *this* graphic?"

The salesman checked the order. "It is what you ordered—an 18' graphic."

Notice the difference? I accidentally ordered eighteen *feet* (18'), when I wanted eighteen *inches* (18"). You might be involved in an industry that does not use those marks to distinguish feet and inches. Trust me, the difference is tremendous and costly if we don't know, define, and *use* Terms correctly.

Everything Changes With the Terms and Definitions

Individuals, Trades, and even entire nations can be Transformed (positively or negatively) by their use of Terms and how they define them.

If you pursue a career as a framer (carpentry), a hip, valley, and cripple will have meaning. You will need to know the cripple extends between a hip and valley rafter at right angles. A cripple jack abuts either a ridge or plate. The heel and side cut will be needed at a cripple and jack rafter. How quickly were you lost, even using English? Your success, as you pursue your new Target/dream will be supported by the Terms you know and use properly in that industry.

Would medical personnel define hip and cripple differently? For five years I met weekly with two physicians, Robert Jackson (Family Practice) and John Thornburg (Radiology). Sometimes they would tell of an interesting case and I found myself unable to understand the conversation. I would teasingly say, "Hold on, let me get my medical dictionary; it's in the car." The Terms contained an entirely new world of information that I was unable to understand, but they were functioning There with ease.

For us to join them, we would need a new foundation—built on Terms.

Back to the Destiny of Marckens and Alejandro

Marckens will learn that *two* official languages are present in Haiti: French and Haitian Creole. Almost all Haitians speak Creole, whereas only 10% of the population is bilingual in French. French is the language of most formal situations: schools, newspapers, courts, and official documents. Creole (spoken by 90% of the population) had no written form until the 1940s, or certified grammar until 1976, or an official dictionary until around 2001. Those who speak Creole exclusively, suffer under the inability to understand or communicate in business and legal transactions. Their foundation is weak.

Alejandro will learn that Costa Rica has one official language: Spanish. There are other languages present, but the majority understands the language of business, education, and government. Excellent education has provided a proper foundation for a country of healthy and productive people.

Costa Rica has the highest literacy rate in Central American. Because of the mastery, spoken and written, Costa Ricans can build their lives. In comparison, Haiti has the lowest literacy rate in the western hemisphere, yielding massive poverty. Our thinking, education, and futures have a common foundation—Terms. Our destiny will be built on mastering the Terms of our chosen dreams and Targets

Writing Provides the Foundation for Your Dreams

Habakkuk was a poet of another era. He wrote, "Write the vision, so the herald can run with it." An architect or designer, using universally agreed-upon Terms and definitions, can design a building or machine in Japan. It can be built perfectly in South Dakota. All he and the builders have to agree upon is the definition of the Terms.

Without a written and understood document, building projects can only be conducted at a primitive level. People who live in mud huts with thatched roofs generally only share knowledge orally. There is either no written language or they don't understand it well enough to read, write, and follow the instructions.

Napoleon Hill, the well known motivational writer, penned these words: "Reduce your plan to writing. The moment you complete this, you will have definitely given concrete form to the intangible desire." Writing gives "concrete form" to Thoughts. If we want to be able to remember, communicate, and build, then we must learn to read, write, and understand the Terms of our dreams.

Dr. Mike Zais, superintendent of education for the State of South Carolina, wrote: "For the first time in American history, we are facing the prospect of a generation less literate than their parents."

Haitians find that not being able to read can be difficult. If we don't master the Terms, could we end up without a foundation to build on? Mark Twain said, "The man who does not read is no better than the man who can't." The man who does not know or use the Terms correctly is equally placing himself at a disadvantage.

A SIMPLE OBSERVATION:

Half of the world's population makes less than $10.00 a day.
Half of the world's population cannot read.
Could there be a correlation?

THINGS TO THINK THROUGH:

- When will you take the Time to learn the Terms you need to build your dreams?
- Could nations be Transformed (+/-) by redefining the Terms which uphold their freedoms?
- When will you write your goals (if you have not done so)? Write carefully, for Terms will determine your future.
- We have learned to develop Terms for ideas, thoughts, and concepts which both give and take meaning. "All men are created equal," gives valuable meaning to everyone. Whereas, "slave," "bum," "whore," and "nerd" take value. What is the foundation of the Terms you use?
- What terms do you need to function in your desired Target/Goal?

ANCIENT WRITINGS: "These words I speak to you are not incidental additions to your life, homeowner improvements to your standard of living. They are foundational words, words to build a life on. If you work these words into your life, you are like a smart carpenter who built his house on solid rock. Rain poured down, the river flooded, a tornado hit—but nothing moved that house. It was fixed to the rock."

BOOK: *Read and Grow Rich* by Burke Hedges

I WILL APPLY THIS PRINCIPLE BY: _____

_____

_____

_____

I need a Teacher to help me move from here to there. When I have a Target, the proper Teacher will naturally Transmit the Terms, and appropriate *Technique(s)* to me . . .

CHAPTER E

Technique(s)

Let's take a time machine to 1974. I am sixteen. The grocery store is buggy-to-butt crowded with customers. You will notice it's just a few days before Christmas. This aisle, where mayonnaise, mustard, and olives are stocked is my responsibility. I keep every label facing forward, every jar perfectly in line.

Together, we will re-watch a two-minute *play* where I learn a—Technique—that changed my life.

Occasionally, in this hectic and swarming environment, I receive a *bump*. Actually, that is why I invited you to my aisle—to observe some bumps and watch some ladies. This aisle gives a sixteen-year-old boy *many* opportunities to watch the ladies.

Speaking of—check out *this* one. Her shoes have a small heel, dress is knee-length, hair—a red tint. Accessories—let's call her—well arranged. She is making selections and placing them in a cart pushed by a man that I would assume is her husband. They try to zip between customers and, oh no! It seems he has bumped her heel.

"Wilbur, you clumsy idiot! What the _ _ _ _ do you think you are doing? Why don't you watch where that _ _ _ _ buggy is going?"

I want to get away from her as fast and as far as I can. I am going back to stocking pickles. Take a breath and try to relax with me. That is not the end of the play—just act one.

Here comes our second actress. She is weaving through this crowd like a New York City taxi driver when the impossible, or at least the improbable, takes place. The same "well arranged" woman has been bumped by our second actress.

Wait. I now hear something absolutely unexpected. "That is okay, I understand. I should have been more thoughtful and been out of your way."

Was that the same well-dressed woman who just cursed her husband?

When she realized a stranger had bumped her, she had a complete change of countenance. She is now apologizing for what, seconds ago, brought curses.

I try to turn my attention back to stocking shelves, but my mind is whirling with questions. I am confused.

The response could not have come because of the *people* involved. One was apparently her husband, the other a total stranger.

That lady's response did not come from the *place*. She only moved a few feet.

I could not fathom that her response came from the *circumstance*. She was hit twice in an almost identical manner with a buggy (shopping cart, if you are not from SC).

This scene is replaying in full color in my mind. *Her response did not come from the people, place, or things involved.*

Then, as I stare at the floor, I realize the truth. *That's it . . . she chose . . . she is responsible . . . she is response-able.*

My heart is now racing with excitement.

Wait a minute. That means I, too, have a choice in how I respond. I cannot blame my response on anybody. I live from the inside out. I don't have to be controlled by all the people, places and circumstances of life. If she chose, I can too. I don't have to let the bumps control my life.

I snap back to reality as the apologies are shared, the play ends, and our players exit.

We have to cut our visit short and head back in our time-capsule. We must not only travel back to the present . . . we must travel into the future.

As we travel the *aisles of life*, we are more than likely going to get some bumps.

Actually, if your life is anything like mine, I can guarantee that you will get some undeserved bumps. When you are bumped the next time, remember: Don't blame your response on any*one*, any *place,* or any*thing*. You are response-*able*.

Working This Out

Ben Carson, the doctor mentioned in the Introduction, said, "Growing up where I lived, it was a macho thing to get angry, kick down the wall, and punch in the window. But I came to understand that when you react on impulse like that, it actually is a sign of weakness, because it means that other people and the environment can control you, and I decided that I didn't want to be that easily controlled."

Your mother could have been single, broke, and eighteen. Maybe you have no running water or electricity. Maybe you're *here* is cluttered in abuse. Or maybe your current *here* is fourteen and pregnant. Don't let the circumstance of your conception or current *here* stop you.

Look to O as an example. (You don't even need her first or last name to recognize her). She found herself in *all* of the illustrations mentioned above, but has become North America's only female African-American billionaire.

Ask Oprah; she may have advice on how to unlock your hidden treasures and dreams. Oprah Winfrey started reading at age three while being raised by a grandmother. Do you wonder how a fourteen-year-old pregnant, single girl from Mississippi could be Transformed into one of the wealthiest, most influential philanthropists in American history? Listen to what she says about this key Technique—responsibility. "I don't think of myself as a poor deprived ghetto girl who made good. I think of myself as somebody who, from an early age, knew I was *responsible* for myself, and I had to make good (emphasis added)."

This Is (almost) My Favorite Book

Mickey Hamlet leads a large group of distributors in a multi-level business. While interviewing people who all made over 100,000 dollars a year, he discovered a common denominator. They all read at least one book a week. If reading a book a week (and applying it – Chapter S Toil) will help you earn 100,000 dollars a year, could I recommend it? Let me recommend an easy to read book. This is a good place to start.

Autobiography in Five Chapters

1. I walk down the street.
    There is a deep hole in the sidewalk. I fall in.
    I am lost . . . I am hopeless. It isn't my fault.
    It takes forever to find a way out.
2. I walk down the same street.
    There is a deep hole in the sidewalk.
    I pretend I don't see it. I fall in again.
    I can't believe I'm in the same place.
    But it isn't my fault. It still takes a long time to get out.
3. I walk down the same street.
    There is a deep hole in the sidewalk. I see it is there.
    I still fall in. It's a habit. My eyes are open. I know where I am.
    It *is* my fault. I get out immediately.
4. I walk down the same street.
    There is a deep hole in the sidewalk. I walk around it.
5. I walk down another street.

The sheriff of our county, Chuck Wright, and I were eating lunch. During the conversation, a very public incident came up. A very prominent organization had a staff member involved in a sexual scandal with a teenager. He mentioned talking with one of the management personnel who was very upset. He calmed him with these words. "I can't be responsible for what people do. I can only be held accountable for how I respond."

You will always be controlled by others (positive responses or lack thereof) if you don't learn to think and say, "I am response-*able*, for my responses." Don't give away your freedom because of the way others respond or do not respond to you. Take responsibility for your attitude, behavior and conversation (a-b-c). Take responsibility for the Target you decide to pursue. This Technique is required if you plan on reaching your desired There.

A SIMPLE OBSERVATION:

The next time you want to curse, kick cans, and
create chaos, remember this:

The Last Freedom

We who lived in concentration camps can remember the men
who walked through the huts comforting others, giving away
their last piece of bread.
They may have been few in number, but they offered sufficient
proof that everything can be taken from a man but one thing: the last
of the human freedoms—to choose one's attitude in any given set of
circumstances—to choose one's own way.

~ Viktor Frankl ~
(Man's Search for Meaning)
Written about his time in a Nazi Concentration Camp.

THINGS TO THINK THROUGH:

- Is the Teacher/coach you have selected Transmitting that kind of responsiveness to you? Or do they blame others for their attitude?
- When did the person in the five-chapter autobiography change?
- Are you taking responsibility? If not, how will you (in specific action) start taking responsibility?
- If you have an area of your life (financial/sexual/spiritual etc.) where you are not taking responsibility, do you find yourself struggling in that area? Why?
- When will you start taking responsibility for yourself? How will you do it?

ANCIENT WRITINGS: "I am not saying this because I am in need, for I have learned to be content whatever the circumstances. I know what it is to be in need, and I know what it is to have plenty. I have learned the secret of being content in any and every situation, whether well fed or hungry, whether living in plenty or in want."

BOOK: *Man's Search for Meaning* by Viktor E. Frankl

I WILL APPLY THIS PRINCIPLE BY: _____

_____

_____

_____

I need a Teacher to help me move from here to there. When I have a Target, the proper Teacher will naturally Transmit the Terms, and appropriate Technique(s) to me. When accompanied with *Trust* . . .

CHAPTER F

Trust

In forty years of service, John Wooden coached his UCLA college basketball team to an 885-203 win/lose record. Under his tutelage, UCLA won ten NCAA championships, including seven consecutive (1966-73). In the 1970s, his teams went on an eighty-eight-game winning streak, setting a NCAA record. No other men's coach has come close to this record.

His methods were unconventional, and occasionally he encountered a player who did not want to Trust him. *Sports Illustrated* writer Rick Reilly penned a piece titled, "A Paragon Rising Above the Madness," in 2000 that chronicled what Wooden believed and how he dealt with players.

> You played for him, you played by his rules: Never score without acknowledging a teammate. One word of profanity and you're done for the day. Treat your opponent with respect.
>
> He believed in hopelessly out-of-date stuff that never did anything but win championships. No dribbling behind the back or through the legs. "There's no need," he'd say. No long hair, no facial hair. "They take too long to dry, and you could catch cold leaving the gym."

That one drove his players bonkers. One day, All-America center Bill Walton showed up with a full beard. "It's my right," he insisted. Wooden asked if he believed that strongly. Walton said he did. "That's good, Bill," Coach said. "I admire people who have strong beliefs and stick by them, I really do. We're going to miss you." Walton shaved it right then and there. Now Walton calls once a week to tell Coach he loves him.

Bill Walton was player of the year, three years in college, and led the team in two Division 1 national titles. Wooden knew his ideas were Trustworthy, even if his "star" player had to leave. Few coaches have ever motivated players as well as Wooden. Simply put, Wooden developed a team who Trusted him, followed his instructions, and *won*.

Trusting the Word

If you are going to succeed personally or on a team, you must Trust the people around you. You need to especially Trust those who are older and have shown the ability to succeed. Bill Walton Trusted his own immature thought processes and nearly found himself off the team. Trusting Wooden was the better choice.

Everyone likes to be liked, but Wooden didn't care about being liked as much as Trusted. He taught the members of his team to Trust each other, and to Trust him as their coach. Wooden had to Trust and live according to his own word if his players were going to Trust him, and Wooden did, even if the players did not like him. Find mentors who can take being unpopular.

Trust is indispensable in the process of moving you to your new *there*. Do you Trust the Teachers, mentors, and coaches you have selected or do you murmur when they offer instructions? If you don't Trust your mentor, his words and example will not have the impact they could have.

Of course, not every Teacher is going to offer the correct advice on every occasion. But when that Teacher has a proven track record of success, as well as having your best interest at heart, it would be foolish not to Trust him or her. How Trustworthy is your Teacher? Does he do what he says, when he says, whether he feels like it or not? If so, he is Trustworthy.

Shame Is a Bad Game

Dr. Dennis Humphries, PhD, who is a licensed clinical counselor and adjunct faculty member at Trinity Evangelical Divinity School, says we have the same four questions running through our minds every day when we wake up:

- Who am I? (A question of identity.)
- Why am I here? (A question of purpose/meaning.)
- Where am I going? (A question of direction.)
- Does anyone really love me? (A question of intimacy.)

If your Teachers can answer those questions, giving you instructions and Transmitting the answers naturally, then you will Trust them. Dr. Marlin Elliott (Chapter Q Teach) did that for me. He was one of my college professors and I was safe with him. I could ask him the most ridiculous questions and he would always answer with patience and understanding. He never caused me to feel shame for my inability to know or understand.

If *dumb* questions, awkward manners, or facial features (or anything else) cause you to feel inferior and shamed when interacting with your mentor, consider finding another one who loves and understands you. Shame destroys the sense of self and splinters your identity. It can be as great a threat as sexual and verbal abuse. And it often manifests itself as depression, anxiety, and anger in the person who feels it. Shame certainly causes us to cover our eyes or hide our face. It keeps us from being our best.

When you no longer Trust your Teacher and begin to withdraw from him or her, ask yourself these questions:

- Are you ashamed of something either the Teacher or you have said?
- Have either of you failed to do something you should have done?
- Have either of you failed to communicate the requirements properly?
- Is there anything you have neglected or disrespected in each other?

Your answers will reveal your level of Trust and Trustworthiness. Correcting the problem will help you move in the direction of a healthy, growing relationship. If that Trust is broken, do whatever it takes to be reconciled to your mentor. He is a lifeline for you.

A Lesson in Trust

Shay Griffin worked at my sign shop for many years and is closer than a brother. Once we realized we could Trust each other, I could send him to do anything. One day, he installed a sign for one of our customers. But when he returned to the shop, something was bothering him. I didn't have to prod him for information. He told me he didn't perform the job up to the company's expectation. The next day, he went back and corrected the error. My customer Trusted my company to do the job right. I Trusted Shay. For the process to work, everyone must stay Trustworthy. If Shay had not told me, the product would have failed and the customer would have called. Trust would have been broken (on many fronts) and progress would have stopped until someone restored it.

We've all traveled different paths, but you have to come to a place in your life in which you Trust someone. It might be God, your parents, yourself (that can be dangerous, just ask Bill Walton) your advisors, supervisors, or a Trustworthy Teacher/mentor. Once you connect with a Trusted mentor, you can experience satisfaction with who you are, what you are doing, where you are in life, and who you are with. When that kind of Trust develops, your life will flow. As my father used to say, "I can see it in his eyes. The light just came on." If the light of Trust does not come on, then neither a mentor, this book, nor any other motivational tool will come to your rescue.

Defining Trust

Dr. Billy Graham, an evangelist from the 20th century, spoke to over 200,000,000 people. He tells a story about a tightrope performer whose line spanned the mighty Niagara Falls with a 180-foot drop. Starting on the United States side of the falls, the performer put a wheelbarrow on the wire and pushed it across into Canada. The crowd cheered hysterically.

When the cheering subsided, he asked, "Who believes I can put a man in this wheelbarrow and push him across to America?"

The crowd resumed their cheering.

When the cheering stopped, he simply asked, "Who will get in?"

To say you Trust someone requires action—getting in. If your mentor tells you to mix the compounds, nail the boards with a number eight nail, or weld steel with a tig welder—can you Trust him enough to follow through? Do you follow instructions without complaint? If not, consider getting another *attitude* (this might be the best place to start), mentor, or dream. You won't grow and flow without Trust.

When you find someone you Trust, someone who understands the process and can help you, you should grab every idea they have to offer. Are you in a Trust relationship with your mentor? If so, you will find he can pull the treasures hidden within you to the surface.

A SIMPLE OBSERVATION:

Trust means climbing into the wheelbarrow.

THINGS TO THINK THROUGH:

- Are your Teachers so committed to Trusted methods that they are willing to hold to them, even if they have to "miss you"?
- Do your Teachers keep their word?
- Do you live in such a way that people will Trust you? How so?
- Do you Trust those in authority over you?
- If someone were to pull your Teacher aside and ask him how Trustworthy you are, what would your mentor say about you?

ANCIENT WRITINGS: "Trust in the LORD with all your heart and lean not on your own understanding."

BOOK: *Mr. Littlejohn's Secrets to A Lifetime of Success* by Pat Williams (This book is out of print – be Tenacious and find it).

I WILL APPLY THIS PRINCIPLE BY: _____

_____

_____

_____

I need a Teacher to help me move from here to there. When I have a Target, the proper Teacher will naturally Transmit the Terms and appropriate Technique(s) to me. When accompanied with Trust, this *Training* will . . .

CHAPTER G

Training

My friend, Luis Rodriguez, grew up in the Dominican Republic speaking Spanish. However, he speaks English so well; you would think English was his native tongue. When I asked Luis how he learned English, he said, "Through my teen years, I was a faithful fan of the TV show *Friends* for ten seasons, when I realized, I can speak English." What other Training did he receive? What else did he learn? Worldviews? Attitudes toward sex? Social skills? Can you be in the company of another without being influenced and Trained on many different levels?

From Passive Learning, to Mimicking, to Mastery

My friend and singer, Caroline Reid, introduced me to Matias Mariani, an up-and-coming opera singer. Always interested in how people move from *here* to *there*, I asked Matias about his Training. He granted me the following interview.

How did you acquire your love for music?

Through my mother. She is a singer-songwriter. I grew up surrounded by music. From birth, my mother would play classical music when she would put me to sleep. Throughout the day, there would always be music playing or she would be singing and playing her guitar.

How did that musical foundation Transform you into a singer?

Once in the U.S., I began to sing in the school choir at McCracken Elementary. It was a wonderful experience and it was my favorite class. At that point music was not my passion, but it brought me great joy and it made my day complete.

Can you explain how your appreciation for music grew?

During high school I was a big fan of Andrea Bocelli. I sang along to his *Sogno* album. That was as classical as singing got for me—other than trying to imitate The Three Tenors. Actually, I first stumbled upon The Three Tenors in 1992 while watching TV. I was seven years old at that time and when I heard those voices I thought it was the coolest thing. From that day on, the big guy with the beard became my mentor as I tried to imitate him.

How did music become your passion?

During my senior year in high school, my choir Teacher, Dr. John Moody, inspired a dream. He assigned me a piece to learn for the school's concerto competition. The piece was *Una furtiva lagrima*. I loved singing, but I had not experimented with an operatic voice. YouTube or iTunes did not exist, so I did my research the old fashioned way—at the library. I checked out a CD of Pavarotti and I learned the piece.

Dr. Moody asked me to stay after school to rehearse in preparation for my audition. I sang the piece with my everyday voice. He thanked me and began to call the next person. I stopped him and said with a heavy accent, "Would you like me to sing it like Pavarotti?" He agreed and I sang it "a la Pavarotti."

He liked it. "I think you should sing it like that," he said. I won the concerto competition. At the end of the year I performed the piece with the school's orchestra. Believe me; it does not get any better for a kid to sing his first solo, his first aria, with an orchestra.

Dr. Moody continued to encourage me to take lessons and that is how I met my next Teacher, Dr. Valerie MacPhail at Converse College. Lessons became my favorite part of the week and slowly, but surely, singing became an integral part of my life. I sang for countless productions. At each performance my love for opera increased and slowly a dream took shape—to sing opera for life!

Are you still passionate, as you live out your dream?

Today the dream is a reality and I am blessed to be able *to do what I love*. What a great feeling it is to be on stage connecting with the audience. What a humbling, life-changing experience to have people come to hear me sing. Not only have I found music, but I found myself through music—all thanks to an after-school activity. Gene, I don't consider my Teachers as just Teachers, but family. They have changed and shaped my life. Also, God. I strongly believe God gave me a talent and talents are meant to be shared. How selfish of me it would be not to share the gift of music with the world. Music brings comfort and joy, especially to those who need it most. I feel blessed and grateful to God for he has given me the privilege of sharing with the world something as beautiful and powerful as music.

Matias' life resonates with the power of having "selected" the right parents (however you do that) and good Teachers to Train him.

Trainings Foundation—Beyond the Terms

Richard F. Abrahamson, PhD is the professor of literature for children and adolescents in the College of Education at the University of Houston. In *A Taste of Chicken Soup for the Teacher's Soul* he wrote powerfully of his daughter Beth, on her first day of school.

"Beth can read any children's book you put in front of her," Abrahamson wrote. "She learned reading the way it should be taught. She learned it naturally, snuggled up in her bed with her mother and me reading her stories at naptime, at bedtime, and at cuddling times throughout the day. To Beth, books are synonymous with good times and loving family. Please don't change her love of reading by making the learning of it a burdensome chore. It has taken us all her life to instill in her the joy of books and learning."

How do you know when your Training has taken root and is moving you toward your desired *there*? Matias and Beth lived their lives the way any child ought to—snuggled up with parents while reading a book or playing in the floor listening to a CD. What they didn't realize was they were being Trained at a deeper level—one that would reach their heart. By the time they started school, their habits were similar to the ones their parents exhibited. They looked like their Teachers (parents) and shared their loves. In Time, we will act and "look like" our Teachers.

Sometimes Distance Does Not Matter

I asked Dr. Phil Bence, who teaches online courses for Indiana Wesleyan University, a simple question as I drove him to the airport. "Do you think online courses are as effective as face-to-face instruction?" There was not a moment's hesitation when I heard, "No." He then continued to explain that from his perspective, distance can slow the Training process. When possible, I encourage Training to be done in close proximity.

However, Jonathan Garcia works for Optec Displays. Optec manufactures and services digital message centers. Recently, I had a message center with a slight problem in displaying the messages. I am illiterate when it comes to understanding the Terms and Techniques needed to repair a center, but due to an employee change I was called on to repair it. Over the phone, Jonathan amazed me with this ability to communicate what I needed to know and do. In moments, I was able to comprehend and repair the unit. (I Trusted him, Chapter F.) Be open to whatever knowledge and Training you can gain, even if it is over a CD, the Internet, or phone. The Transformation can still take place and move you towards your Target. But whenever possible, I would suggest, Train with the Trainer.

Choosing the Right Teacher

In the book *Ministering Cross-Culturally: An Incarnational Model for Personal Relationships,* authors Sherwood Lingenfelter and Marvin Mayers describe ten things we learn, besides the language, when we are influenced by others. In every culture there are "unwritten rules" about values, time, judgment, handling crisis, goals, self-worth, money, work, space, and various other human conducts which sway that society. All of those things contribute to our Training and are learned without our consent—naturally.

Due to the nature of my work, I am often asked, "What do you think about XYZ college or university?" Often I have little to no knowledge of the school. So I always answer with questions.

"What does Christi want to do? What is her dream?"

"She wants to be a biologist," the inquirer answers.

"Why don't you take a biology professor from XYZ-U to lunch? *If* he or she is passionate about science and your daughter leaves totally excited about her dream, then you have selected the right college. If they do not instill a greater love and enthusiasm, I would suggest you continue your search. Look until you find a professor who loves life, science, and students. Then let them train Christi."

Luis learned English, Matias' Training gave him a love for music, and Beth's Training gave her a love for reading. What if their *Friends* spoke Swahili?

A SIMPLE OBSERVATION:

Training comes *through* the person, not *from* the person.

THINGS TO THINK THROUGH:

- What are your Teachers Training you to be?
- Based on how your Teacher speaks and lives, what "music" will you sing?
- By what you watched on TV last night, what language are
- you learning? What do you need to "watch" tonight?
- Are you being Trained to do something you love?
- Can you change your destiny by changing who Trains you?

ANCIENT WRITNGS: "Point your kids in the right direction— when they're old they won't be lost."

BOOK: *Seven Laws of Highest Prosperity* by Cecil O. Kemp Jr.

I WILL APPLY THIS PRINCIPLE BY: _____

_____

_____

_____

I need a Teacher to help me move from here to there. When I have a Target, the proper Teacher will naturally Transmit the Terms and appropriate Technique(s) to me. When accompanied with Trust, this Training will influence my *Thoughts*...

CHAPTER H

Thoughts

Daniel Ross had recently been released from prison. He was *nineteen*. He told me he ended up in jail because he made bad decisions with drugs, money, and free Time. However, he had an abundance of confidence, potential, and passion. So I offered him a job selling signs. *Why not?* He needed a fresh start and he had a sales background—*drugs*.

"What would you do with your life if time, contacts, and money were not an object?" I asked him.

I didn't know it at the Time, but that question changed everything for Daniel.

As we gathered to send him to Asia as a missionary many years later, he said, "When Gene asked me that question, I decided to not let any of those things hold me back."

He correctly understood that his life could be *limited* or *liberated* by his Thoughts. He knew if he pursued the right Teachers, studied success, and focused his thinking, he could turn his life around and reap different results.

Author Brian Tracy said, "A major stimulant to creative thinking is focused questions. There is something about a well-worded question that often penetrates to the heart of the matter and triggers new ideas and insights."

Daniel needed someone to ask him the right questions. He had the potential; he just needed a Transformation of his Thought process. Once he realized he didn't need to be limited by his past or his thinking, he didn't let *anything* hold him back. You can follow his progress at WheresDaniel.com.

Every idea, invention, or change starts with a Thought. Napoleon Hill wrote, *Think and Grow Rich*. The first chapter is titled, "Thoughts are things." Hill wrote: "First comes Thought; then organization of that Thought into ideas and plans; then Transformation of those plans into reality. The beginning, as you will observe, is in your imagination."

Jim Rohn has shared his motivational, success-focused messages with more than 6,000 audiences and over five million people. Mr. Rohn asks, "Have you ever wondered how to turn nothing into something? First, in order to turn nothing into something, you've got to start with some ideas and imagination. Now, it might be hard to call ideas and imagination nothing; but how tangible are those ideas? That is a bit of a mystery. I don't believe ideas that can be turned into a hotel, ideas that can be turned into an enterprise, ideas that can be turned into a new vaccine, or ideas that can be turned into some miracle product, should be called nothing. But tangibly, you have nothing. Interesting! Think of it, ideas that become so powerful in your mind and in your consciousness that they seem real to you even before they become tangible. Imagination that is so strong, you can actually see it."

Jim Rohn was born to an Idaho farming family in the mid-1900's. At the age of twenty-five, he was struggling financially and working paycheck to paycheck. He met his mentor, John Earl Shoaff, and over the next six years became a millionaire by pursuing, listening to, and following Mr. Shoaff's advice. He learned to turn nothing into something by taking Thoughts and joining them to passion and action.

Two Shoe Salesmen

Two shoe salesmen arrived in Africa. Upon arriving, they decided to double their efforts. One would go north and the other south. Four days later, the home office received two, almost identical, telegrams.

"I have been in Africa four days. No one wears shoes. Please send me a ticket home, immediately."

The other telegram arrived moments later. "I have been in Africa four days. No one wears shoes. Please send me 10,000 pairs of shoes—immediately."

The facts, location, and circumstances were identical. The difference? Thought process. One salesman saw people who didn't wear shoes and thought the situation was pointless, while the other one saw his circumstances as an untapped market in which everybody was a potential customer (and he could make a fortune). Thought patterns determine destiny.

Do you desire to stay where you are—living in a shoeless world? If so, then don't challenge yourself—don't change your mentors and thinking. Your tomorrow will be spent right *here*, shoeless.

Bernard Baruch, financier, said: "During my eighty-seven years, I have witnessed a whole succession of technological revolutions. But none of them has done away with the need for character in the individual or the ability to think."

Plant Better Thoughts

My brother Ernie and his late wife Pat have twins, Pam and Julie. Soon after the girls started school, they bounced off the bus one fall evening with great excitement. "Daddy, Daddy, today we got to sit in the back of the bus with the sixth graders. If we can sit back there, we will soon know everything."

Sixth graders don't know *everything*, but a *first* grader doesn't understand where to find a Teacher. Unfortunately, many people don't pursue the right people to influence their lives. Do we understand who we need to pursue and which people should be influencing our lives?

Chapter U provides a Test which can help you understand if the road you are on is really where you want to be. You might want to take that Test now. But I have a question for you first. Are you experiencing life as you desire or are you living vicariously through a reality show or someone else's dream? Are you learning from "sixth graders" and following their advice? If so, what are you going to do about it?

Earl Nightingale wrote *The Strangest Secret*. He says the brain does not care what you plant in it any more than a field does. Whatever you plant will grow. If you want your Thought life to grow and flourish in a certain area, it is up to you to plant the right seeds.

Clear the Weeds

Ken Medema is a world class piano player. What makes him great? As talented as he is, you might be even more impressed to hear that he is blind. He began playing at age five. His parents pursued a Teacher who taught him to improvise.

During his concert at Southern Wesleyan University, Ken said, "Every time I learned a piece, my teacher would tell me, 'Now you improvise in your style.' So music became a second language."

Ken uses this foundation of musical expression to achieve his dream. He could use his blindness as an excuse to be, and have, and do nothing. But he didn't, and doesn't, thanks in large part to his mother. She could have Thought, *Ken's blind, we will have to care for him forever.* But she chose to think, *He can be great and we will help him get there.* She did not let the natural feelings one could have with a child who has special needs control her. She put *weed-killer* on the weeds and nurtured the seeds which produced the harvest she wanted.

Ken went on to receive a master's from Michigan State University to enhance his abilities. You can hear a song of Ken's at 21-Ts.com regarding Chapter O Time,

"Thoughts become things but only if there's action behind them," says business trainer and coach, Hilton Johnson, Your idea can become a tangible "thing" to touch, smell, and experience, if you will kill the excuses and nurture the positive seeds (Thoughts).

Weeds Are Real, but They Can Be Weeded

W. Woodworth wrote:

> Your mind is a garden,
> Your Thoughts are the seeds.
> You can plant flowers.
> Or you can plant weeds.

Some people face mental struggles which are not of their doing, like my daughter with Down syndrome. However, some people have planted weeds. Jeff Burgess, my nephew, had a mental mountain to move. He learned the phrase: "Change what you listen to. It can change who you are." He reviewed the music on his iPod and made some changes. "When I took out the negative music and replaced it with positive music, I came out on top," he told me. Terms and Tools, like Technology, are neither good nor bad in themselves. It's what we choose to play, hear, and do with them that is good or bad.

Benjamin Disraeli, the 1st Earl of Beaconsfield said: "Nurture your mind with great thoughts for you will never go any higher than you think."

I memorized this poem of Fanny Crosby years ago. She wrote these words when she was eight years old:

Oh, what a happy soul I am,
although I cannot see!

I am resolved that in this world
contented I will be.

How many blessings I enjoy,
that other people don't

To weep and sigh because I'm blind,
I cannot and I won't!

"Every life experience will make you better or bitter," my South Dakota friend Evelyn McFadden says. Can you shake off your negative thoughts and move on? Can you order shoes in a shoeless place?

A SIMPLE OBSERVATION:

Every dream will become a reality or die in the dust
depending on your Thoughts and actions.

THINGS TO THINK THROUGH:

- Thoughts will either freeze or free you. Are your Thoughts free or frozen?
- There are various people "supposedly" responsible for this statement, so my source is uncertain. "Some men have thousands of reasons why they cannot do what they want to, when all they need is one reason why they can." What is your one reason to move forward?
- David Ring, motivational speaker says, "I have cerebral palsy, but palsy doesn't have me." What has you?
- Do you have an "ailment" that you believe is stopping you from living the life you've always dreamed? Over the next thirty days, read biographies of people who overcame their challenges. Apply their Thoughts and actions to your situation. Are you willing to take that challenge?
- Think about the music, movies, television shows, magazines, and websites you visit. Are they affecting you positively or negatively? What do you plan to do about it?

ANCIENT WRITINGS: "For as he thinks within himself, so he is."

BOOKS: *The Magic of Thinking Big* by David J. Schwartz, *Acres of Diamonds* by Russell Conwell, and *The Strangest Secret* by Earl Nightingale

I WILL APPLY THIS PRINCIPLE BY:_____

_____

_____

_____

I need a Teacher to help me move from here to there. When I have a Target, the proper Teacher will naturally Transmit the Terms and appropriate Technique(s) to me. When accompanied with Trust, this Training will influence my Thoughts and help me understand the *Tools* . . .

CHAPTER I

Tools

Richard and I had cleaned the meat department like robots, working in perfect timing, a hundred times. But on this night Richard's rhythm was off. In two thoughtless moments, a Tool designed to serve mankind twisted and produced something beyond recognition—shreds—at the end of his arm.

We had been taught how to use, care for, and clean the Tools in the meat department. We knew how to disassemble and clean the Tools for health department inspections. But that night Richard forgot one detail. The grinder has a thirty-five-horsepower motor. That motor pushes large pieces of meat with ease.

The meat flows through a shaft as it is compressed and forced through small holes. The end product from this massive tool is hamburger.

Richard knew the routine and a few shortcuts. He started disassembling the meat grinder by removing a cover. He bypassed a safety switch and hit the start button. This forced out the remaining good meat so he could accelerate the cleaning process. He turned the machine off, but grabbed the gear thinking he could stop the machine quicker with his grip. He was wrong. The momentum could *not* be easily stopped. Richard's hand went through a couple of revolutions as the motor ground to a stop.

Richard failed to use a great machine as the manufacturer had intended it to be used, and the results were disastrous. The manufacture designed this machine to make hamburger. His hand went partially through that process. Even though he had numerous surgeries, he still cannot use his right hand properly.

Building a Foundation

In ninth-grade shop class, our Teacher entered the room and began to explain all the Tools we were admiring. "This saw will . . . this Tool rotates the wood so you can make table legs, lamps, and . . . this is a drill press, you can make multiple holes." The process began with the Teacher describing each of the Tools thoroughly and its *intended* use.

He helped us form a foundation upon which we could build the understanding required to know how to use them. We learned what each Tool could and could not do, and how to operate them safely. After passing many safety tests and gaining an appreciation for each Tool and its awesome power, our Teacher taught us how to build simple projects. Eventually, we learned how to make workbenches, lamps, and various other useful products. By the time we moved on to the tenth grade, we had a good working knowledge about the machines. We knew what they could accomplish and how the manufacture intended them to be used.

Understanding Tools

Every occupation has Tools, whether pencils, cranes, or airplanes. We all need something in our hands to assist us in the process of Transformation.

There is nothing wrong with a shovel and, at times, it is 100% necessary. Tools are necessary whether they are small or large, expensive or not. You must learn their value and their intended purpose. As you look into your ideal future, are you becoming familiar with the Tools required for that Trade?

Rich Is Rich for a Reason

Rich DeVos is *rich*. He is co-owner of Amway and a professional sports team (Orlando Magic). He has a relationship with his God, is respected by his peers, and his wife and children love him. That combination makes a man rich in all areas. He created an outstanding Training product, including a book, videos, and live seminars called: *Compassionate Capitalism*. The concepts he explains show that the man who is a capitalist with compassion truly makes economies and nations thrive. He uses a simple equation:

MW = NR + HE X T

- **MW** – Material Welfare – the process of producing and/or distributing capital.
- **NR** – Natural Resources – we are all dependant on natural recourses (wool, water, and wood).
- **HE** – Human Energy – sheep don't give wool and the rain does not collect on its own. To Transform those items to a usable form, human energy is required.
- Then we have the **X** factor – **T**ools.

In Peru, a man will carry 100 pounds of wood on his back. In North America, a man gets in a truck and carries 40,000 pounds of wood while listening to the stereo in air conditioning. The difference is just the Tool.

If people don't have access to natural resources and cannot own Tools, production falls. This is one of the curses of Marxist socialism.

DeVos writes: "Two things always happen when the natural resources and Tools are owned by the people: they last longer and they are used more effectively,"

When someone other than ourselves (the state, for example) owns the Tool (such as the tractor to mow road banks), it can be easy to neglect the care and maintenance. However, if we have worked, saved, and bought the machine ourselves, we will maintain, clean, and use it to its maximum potential. In Time, the man who *really* owns the Tool will control the money. Free enterprise is a great Tool itself to promote ownership of Tools and freedom.

The designing and improvement of Tools has always been important for the advancement of society. Two men can cut wood with axes, hatchets, and mauls, and cut a tree a day, if the tree is small. Or they could use chainsaws and hydraulic splitters and cut a few trees a day. They might also consider using huge logging equipment. They can cut, strip, and load dozens of trees per hour. They will be at the mill before the men with axes take a lunch break.

Tools have tremendous power to advance but also change society. Tools have no character. They take on the character of the owner. An inspirational and motivational writer uses letters, words, paper, ink, and printers. Those same Tools in the hands of a child pornographer produce drastically different results. Meat grinders do not care *whose* meat is passing through; they simply grind meat.

The Issue Is Intent

Dennis McIntee is a business coach, trainer, and friend. He explains a process of taking all the Terms and information Transmitted to us (knowledge), and being able to Transform it into action.

As Dennis leads a workshop, he will write on the left side of his dry erase board: **KNOWLEDGE.**

He defines knowledge as the accumulation of all the information you have received.

In school you attended classes in which you had an iPad or text books. You wrote notes and even took them home (hopefully to study). You took Tests related to that material, and if you are like most of us, you never reviewed the material again. I have put in lots of Time, energy, miles, and red eyes, only to do little or nothing with the new knowledge. Therefore, no Transformation took place.

On the other side of his board Dennis writes: **ACTION.**

KNOWLEDGE   **ACTION**

We all must take action to accomplish anything. My "little" girl just drove out of the driveway for the first time. She got her license November

21, 2012. All of the Teachers, Terms, and knowledge she received regarding driving went into action. Much of that Transmittal process was caught as she watched me. Thank God, I drive under the speed limit. Still, I pray she is using that knowledge and is at Sarah's house. I want to remember today, so I took a picture with her, the car, and my credit card (you can see it at 21-Ts.com).

This is where Dennis explains that countless hours of study can yield little to no Transformation. What other factor do we need between knowledge and action to succeed? Dennis will write in the center of the board: **INTENTION.** The board will then read:

KNOWLEDGE   INTENTION   ACTION

The person who reaches their goal is not necessarily the one who attends the seminar, makes an A or wins the contest. One of the deciding factors for completing the Transformation process is who will take the knowledge Transmitted (Truth hopefully – Chapter M) from the Teacher and with passion and purpose *intentionally* use it in an appropriate way. That is the person who will win at the end of the day. The deciding factor is your answer to, "What is your intention?" I will repeat. Without an intentional plan, passion, and purpose applied to the knowledge, the action will not take place. Transformation and success will not have an opportunity to grow.

What do we intend to do with this new information? Intention is one of the best Tools to have in our briefcase or toolbox. Why read a book, go to college, or spend Time with a Teacher if there is not going to be life change? A Transformation that yields change and produces new results in the way we Think and live will infect our family and, eventually, the community in which we live.

I don't know what Tools you have or which ones you need to acquire. However, I know nothing will happen until you use the Tool of intention. Find the right Teacher who can show which Tools to acquire, use them with good intentions, as the manufacture recommended and you'll reap the rewards. Remember Richard's hand.

A SIMPLE OBSERVATION:

Tools are the multiplying factor if you intend to use them properly.
(Intention is a mega multiplier.)

THINGS TO THINK THROUGH:

- What Tools (even unused notebooks) do you need to dust off so you can put the knowledge into practice?
- What do you intend to do with this chapter?
- Who could Teach you to focus your intentions?
- What is in your hand? A pen? A keyboard? A hammer? Are you using it as the manufacture intended?
- Tools are neutral. Intent can be positive or negative. Are you using your Tools with the right intention?

ANCIENT WRITINGS: "Whatever your hand finds to do, do it with all your might, for in the grave, where you are going, there is neither working nor planning nor knowledge nor wisdom."

BOOK: *Compassionate Capitalism* by Rich DeVos

I WILL APPLY THIS PRINCIPLE BY:_____

_____

_____

_____

I need a Teacher to help me move from here to there. When I have a Target, the proper Teacher will naturally Transmit the Terms and appropriate Technique(s) to me. When accompanied with Trust, this Training will influence my Thoughts and help me understand the Tools and *Technology* . . .

CHAPTER J

Technology

Nathaniel Gaffney and I were enjoying the stunning scenery as we twisted and turned our way through the mountain road. A.D. Parks, a teenager accompanying us, was busy texting and surfing on his phone. We were going camping in a remote area of South Carolina where the views are marvelous.

"No Service," A.D. said, charging the air with this abrupt and panicked interruption to our solitude. After finally giving up, he stared out the window at the mountains. Disgusted, he moaned, "What are we going to do?"

Nathaniel, who is also a teenager, laughed and offered, "Enjoy the water, fish, and go for a hike. We're going to cook trout on the fire tonight!"

A.D. was quiet as we drove to the campsite, but he couldn't hold it in long. "What do the teenagers do here? They don't have Wi-Fi."

Nathaniel then described "dial up" service (something from another age and foreign to A.D.).

Technology is here to stay in its ever-changing forms. Will we be able to keep pace, adjust, and use it to our best possible advantage? Or will we allow it to zap our Time as we bounce from one social media site to another?

Bobby Lost His Job

We will look at Bobby Bevill and his situation more (Chapter L Trade), but for now let me say, Bobby has a nice job overseeing over forty service technicians for Davis Services (a heating and air conditioning company). As we discussed his chosen degree and career, Bobby told me, "I have a computer engineering degree."

My face must have wrinkled as I asked, "Why are you servicing air conditioners?"

"I earned my degree over thirty years ago," Bobby said. "Then I served my country for four years in the military. When I was discharged, I found my knowledge was obsolete."

Technology has created advancements, advantages, and activities which would have been totally impossible just two years ago. However, even though our society has many more "gadgets" to play and work with, are we really living more abundantly and vibrantly? Bobby's story happened over thirty years ago, back when Technology moved much slower than today. What you know today may (or will) be out of date by next year (or next week).

Observations to Consider

1. Technology has made many conveniences affordable for the masses.
2. Technology controls almost every business. Actually, it controls almost *everything,* from simple pens to airplanes, and if you are not careful . . . you.
3. Technology in a cell phone allows you to bank, take pictures, surf the web, and discover more technology.

But . . .

1. Do you have to have your cell phone with you all the time?
2. Technology can be beneficial, but learning to enjoy the Technology we own may be better.
3. Technology is designed to un-clutter and un-complicate our lives. Has it?

Technology Giver or Taker

My editor, Lee Warren, interviewed David Mickey Evans recently. He wrote the movie *The Sandlot* (set in 1962 about boys who played pickup baseball). The movie became a huge success after it was released on VHS. His movie was released in 1993 and it has sold more copies every year it has been out. Evans has been touring the country to promote the 20th Anniversary Edition DVD that was recently released. Lee asked him why his movie still resonates with people.

Mr. Evans replied: "It took place in the last great innocent year in American history, right before Kennedy was assassinated and everything went to hell in a hand basket," Evans said. "And I think all of us, no matter how old we are, we want that. We want that kind of freedom and adventure."

When I was thirteen in 1971, my mother did not get nervous when she could not reach me in two hours (or two minutes). I would play in the woods, hike, and hunt miles from the house. Life was relaxed and ran at a different pace.

What I am describing here is a more innocent time period in our nation's history. We cannot go back and I understand that, but I want you to really live, *now*.

Tonight I sat outside of a Best Buy as my daughter bought a new and improved i-thing-a-ma-jig. I can call her, know who she is talking with, and where she is located—at any moment. Still, some parents are nervous if they can't reach their children on the second ring.

Don't let the stress factor that might be true for an older generation, deter your love for Technology. For many of you it is invigorating. Learning new Technology comes naturally for you because you have grown up with it (Chapter A). For us *older* people, some Technology can be a pain—something to be learned before we get the full benefit. It causes us (forty-and-up types) literal headaches and fits of anger (but not if we are response-*able*). But a fifteen-year-old pushes the slider to the right, hits settings, and has the entire thing set up within minutes. This is exactly what happens when Apple releases a new system. Older people throw a fit. Younger people rejoice.

Louis C.K., an Emmy and Grammy award-winning professional stand-up comedian did an interview on CONAN. He demonstrated how young people are always looking down, texting, and not making eye contact. He also shared how someone using text messaging could call someone fat and not feel any regret, where they would not do the same in person. The phones are taking away the ability to sit with someone and be personable, relating to others as you should. So he solved that problem in his home. He did not let his children have cell phones.

Modern Technology has made us believe we can't live or function without it. But when Technology controls our Time, it is controlling our life. Even when we have an abundance of "gadgets," will we really be alive?

Two of my sons, Andrew and Stephen, built a fire in the woods with our friend Robbie. I walked into the woods to visit them that night. There they were—texting.

"If you three are texting each other, I'm going to open a can of Whoop Butt!" (Actually, that's not what I said, but you get the idea.) I was smiling, but it was sad. The weather was perfect, they had a fire, and they had a chance to enjoy the moment. But they weren't present in the moment. Technology was mastering the moment and taking them away to another place.

In his book, *Time Traps: Proven Strategies for Swamped Salespeople*, Todd Duncan makes this observation, "The only thing rising on the wings of Technology is frustration."

I am not certain that is true, but his point can be considered.

If we are going to keep up with the Technological overload we are experiencing, I think we should use some of Duncan's' suggestions. I am only using a few of his thoughts with brief explanations. (Get his book for a more details.)

Shorten the leash. Turn off your phone. Go to the bathroom in peace.

Don't keep four computers and only use one.

Test your gadgets' efficiency. If the newer is lighter, stronger, and more efficient—go for it.

If you have something that works for you. Use it.

Duncan asks, "Do we stay on top with Technology or is Technology on top of us?"

How Technology Controlled My Life

Recently, I stopped in Central, SC. I had been there a hundred times and drove there without reviewing directions. My next stop was Belton, SC, and I had no idea how to get there from Central. I turned on the GPS, typed in 19303 Highway 20, Belton, SC, and never thought about where I was going after that.

After many turns and twists, *I woke up*—in Belton. However, I had let Technology control my responses. Technology was designed to help us, but there are days when I wonder . . . is it helping or controlling? Again, that will be up to us and our choice in how we respond.

Without Technology this book would not be possible. Where is the balance? I pray we find it for I believe we need to be response-*able* in this area as well. Bill Gates said, "Technology is just a Tool. In terms of getting the kids working together and motivating them, the Teacher is the most important."

We are back to this basic truth: You need a good Teacher. Choose that Teacher carefully while you use Technology as it was intended to be used.

A SIMPLE OBSERVATION:
Learn to enjoy what you have before you become discontent about not owning the next invention.

THINGS TO THINK THROUGH
- How will you allow Technology to influence you?
- What Technology do you need to really live?
- Do we really want Technology to control our every move?
- Do we need all the gadgets?
- What Technology will you use to design your life and career?

ANCIENT WRITINGS: "Then he said to them, 'Watch out! Be on your guard against all kinds of greed; a man's life does not consist in the abundance of his possessions.'"

BOOK: *The Precious Present* by Spencer Johnson, M.D.

I WILL APPLY THIS PRINCIPLE BY:_____

_____

_____

_____

I need a Teacher to help me move from here to there. When I have a Target, the proper Teacher will naturally Transmit the Terms and appropriate Technique(s) to me. When accompanied with Trust, this Training will influence my Thoughts and help me understand the Tools and Technology, along with the *Tricks* . . .

CHAPTER K

Tricks

Tamerlane was a 14th century Asian Emperor. He led his troops to countless victories. However, Tamerlane didn't win every day. This day was one of them. The enemy had overcome his men and they are searching for him and his troops. He lies alone, covered in piles of corn stalks in a deserted barn.

With little hope, an ant catches Tamerlane's eye. He has nothing to do but fear being discovered—and killed, so he begins to watch the ant. The tiny ant tries to carry a large piece of corn up a wall. He tries and tries and tries and tries. Finally, realizing the ant would not give up on this "impossible" task, Tamerlane starts counting the attempts: one, two, three . . . ten . . . twenty . . . forty . . . and on to sixty-one attempts. Each Time the ant tries to carry the corn up the vertical wall, it looses its grip on the corn and it tumbles down. At each failed attempt, the ant goes down to retrieve the corn and starts up again: sixty-two, sixty-three, sixty-four, sixty-five . . . sixty-nine, but on the seventieth attempt, the ant reached the goal. Sixty-nine times he tried. Sixty-nine times he failed. But on the seventieth attempt—he did not only try—the corn went over the top.

Here in this deserted, lonely, and forgotten corn crib, Tamerlane knows if an ant can do it, so can he. And he did. He decided that victory would be his, despite the odds! He leaves the desolate corn crib, reorganizes his troops, and wins in the end.

Scared? Depressed? Uncertain what he was going to do? Sure. But he knew the Trick. That moment with the ant changed his life and the course of history. Alexander the Great is the only Emperor to conquer more land than Tamerlane.

This story is not about Tamerlane. It is not about an ant. It is about you. On our road to winning the war of Transforming your idea into reality, you and I may lose a few battles too. We might find ourselves beside Tamerlane, scared and covered in corn stalks, which provide little protection from men with clubs and spears. Let's not waste the moment. What can we learn *here* to help us rise to fight again, as we move to *there*?

The Transformation we are working toward does not occur in a vacuum of dreams and wishes. Chapter S Toil is yet to be explored, but there is nothing easy about being Transformed. If it were easy, more people would do it. Yes, we all could—but the *Trick* is in the willingness to rise again and persevere.

This Trick is universally true for any Trade. You need to find the specific Terms, Techniques, Technology, and Tools for your precise Trade. But to find those ingredients in any Trade, Tenacity is the Trick.

- Tenacity: Tending to stick firmly to any decision, plan, or opinion without changing or doubting it.
- You may prefer perseverance, which is defined: Steady and continued action or belief, usually over a long period and especially despite difficulties or setbacks.

This is the Trick to solve so many challenges. Grab on, hold on, and keep on until you succeed. Just a pure, dogged, obstinate, face-in-the-wind determination.

Try-Fail-Adjust—Try-Fail-Adjust

This Trick cannot be taught. It is a matter of the heart. I have a poster in my office which reads: Try, Fail, Adjust—Try, Fail, Adjust—Try, Fail, Adjust. The letters get smaller and smaller until the bottom reads: SUCCESS. That is Tenacity in action.

Calvin Coolidge, the thirtieth president of the United States, summed it up well: "Nothing in the world can take the place of persistence. Talent will not; nothing is more common than unsuccessful men with talent. Genius will not; unrewarded genius is almost a proverb. Education will not; the world is full of educated derelicts. Persistence and determination are omnipotent."

The Trick is Tenacity—perseverance. Observe the dates, occupations, and nationality as you read the quotes below.

- "If you add a little to a little, and then do it again, soon that little shall be much." – Hesiod (Greek poet, scholar, 750-650 BC)
- "It does not matter how slowly you go as long as you do not stop." – Confucius (Chinese teacher, 551-479 BC)
- "Dripping water hollows out stone, not through force, but through persistence." – Ovid (Roman Poet, 43 BC-17 AD)
- "He conquers who endures." – Persius (Italian, 100 AD)
- "Even after a bad harvest there must be sowing." – Seneca (Roman stoic philosopher, 4 BC-AD 65)
- "If your determination is fixed, I do not counsel you to despair. Few things are impossible to diligence and skill. Great works are performed not by strength, but perseverance." – Samuel Johnson (author, poet, and moralist, 1709-84)
- "Great things are not done by impulse, but by a series of small things brought together." – Vincent Van Gogh (artist, born in Holland, 1853-1890)
- "Let me not pray to be sheltered from dangers, but to be fearless in facing them. Let me not beg for the stilling of my pain, but for the heart to conquer it." – Rabindranath Tagore, (India, poet, playwright, novelist, 1861-1941)
- "Permanence, perseverance, and persistence in spite of all obstacles, discouragements, and impossibilities: It is this that in all things distinguishes the strong soul from the weak." – Thomas Carlyle (writer, historian, and teacher 1795-1881)
- "I do not think that there is any other quality so essential to success of any kind as the quality of perseverance. It overcomes

almost everything, even nature." – John D. Rockefeller (American industrialist, founded Standard Oil, 1839-1937)

- "Perseverance is a great element of success. If you only knock long enough and loud enough at the gate, you are sure to wake up somebody." – Henry Wadsworth Longfellow (educator, poet, and national literary figure 1807-1882)

- "One of the commonest mistakes and one of the costliest is thinking that success is due to some genius, some magic— something or other which we do not possess. Success is generally due to holding on, and failure to letting go. You decide to learn a language, study music, take a course of reading, and train yourself physically. Will it be success or failure? It depends upon how much pluck and perseverance that word 'decide' contains. The decision that nothing can overrule, the grip that nothing can detach, will bring success. Remember the Chinese proverb, 'With time and patience, the mulberry leaf becomes satin.'" – Maltbie Davenport Babcock (clergyman, song writer, poet, 1858-1901)

- "The miracle, or the power, that elevates the few is to be found in their industry, application, and perseverance under the prompting of a brave, determined spirit." – Mark Twain (writer, entertainer, 1835-1910)

- "In the confrontation between the stream and the rock, the stream always wins—not through strength but by perseverance." – (H. Jackson Brown, Jr., American, 1940- present)

- "When things go wrong, don't go with them." – Elvis Presley (singer, businessman, 1935-1977)

- "If I had to select one quality, one personal characteristic that I regard as being most highly correlated with success, whatever the field, I would pick the trait of persistence. Determination. The will to endure to the end, to get knocked down seventy times and get up off the floor saying. 'Here comes number seventy-one!'" – Richard M. DeVos (American businessman, 1926- present)

Are you tired of reading about tenacity? Is perseverance boring? Are you ready to jump to the next chapter and get to the "good" stuff? Please stop.

Let's agree on something before we go any further. The Transformation and climb required to reach our goals, whatever they may be, will take a lot longer and be a lot harder than reading these words. This chapter is *long* for a reason. I hope we both decide to climb, scratch, and claw through whatever we have to—to reach our dream. This is just the start. Our back, legs, eyes, ears, hands, and fingers will hurt before we reach our goals. Keep reading. Stick to this tenaciously.

- "I am not judged by the number of times I fail, but by the number of times I succeed; and the number of times I succeed is in direct proportion to the number of times I fail and keep trying." – Tom Hopkins (sales trainer)
- "A little more persistence, a little more effort, and what seemed hopeless failure may turn to glorious success." –Elbert Hubbard (publisher, artist, and philosopher,1856-1915)
- "The person who makes a success of living is the one who sees his goal steadily and aims for it unswervingly. That is dedication." – Cecil B. De Mille (film producer and director, 1881-1959)
- "It's not that I'm so smart, it's just that I stay with problems longer." "I think and think for months and years. Ninety-nine times, the conclusion is false. The hundredth time I am right." – Albert Einstein, (thinker, physicist, 1879 –1955)
- "You're never a loser until you quit trying." – Mike Ditka (former NFL player, television commentator, and coach 1939-present)
- "Stubbornly persist and you will find that the limits of your stubbornness go well beyond the stubbornness of your limits." – Robert Brault (singer-tenor, 1963-present)
- "What counts is not necessarily the size of the dog in the fight— it's the size of the fight in the dog." – General Dwight Eisenhower (thirty-fourth President of the United States, 1890-1969)
- "Perseverance is the hard work you do after you get tired of doing the hard work you already did." – Newt Gingrich (former congressman, 1943-present)
- "You can't go through life quitting everything. If you're going to achieve anything, you've got to stick with something." – From the

television show *Family Matters*
- "There is no telling how many miles you will have to run while chasing a dream." – Author Unknown
- "There's only one way to succeed in anything, and that is to give it everything." – Vincent Lombardi (coach of the Green Bay Packers, 1913-1970)
- "I will persist until I succeed. Always will I take another step. If that is of no avail I will take another, and yet another. In truth, one step at a time is not too difficult. I know that small attempts, repeated, will complete any undertaking." – Og Mandino (author whose books sold millions of copies, 1923-1996)
- "If you stand up and be counted, from time to time you may get yourself knocked down. But remember this: A man flattened by an opponent can get up again. A man flattened by conformity stays down for good." – Thomas J. Watson, Jr. (business man, second president of IBM, 1914-1993)
- "When obstacles arise, you change your direction to reach your goal, you do not change your decision to get *there*." –Zig Ziglar (corporate trainer, motivational speaker, 1926-2012) (accent added).

Do you feel that urge to quit reading? Quitting is the easiest thing to do Today. But quitting is a tough memory to live with tomorrow. Are you ready to move on? I want to repeat myself. Reading these few words is nothing compared to what we will go through to reach our Target. Our minds will struggle with self-doubt and our bodies will desire to quit. Our eyes will burn and our bodies will ache before we reach our goals. Actually my fingers are aching. It is 7:09 a.m. on a Saturday morning and I have been here for two hours. You will ache and burn too—but the result is well worth it. Read on, this is just the beginning.

Tamerlane learned the great lesson of perseverance from the ant, and that is something we can repeat. Let Tamerlane, the ant, and King Solomon become our Teachers. King Solomon of Israel wrote: "Go to the ant, consider its ways and be wise." I once acquired an ant colony—in an attempt to gain some of that wisdom. Got them for Christmas. I wanted to learn about ants and thought, *No better way to learn than move a few in with me* (Ah-choo). Those ants did not want to move *in*. Actually they wanted to move *out*. And they did. They moved right out of their aquarium and moved into my house. They bit the family and generally made life miserable. If we hadn't acted response-*able* (Chapter E), life might have spun out of control. So we acted accordingly and moved them OUT.

I have seen a lot of ants, killed a few, been bitten by many, and can't say I learned much wisdom from them. But I will share my limited knowledge/wisdom with you here.

1. God thinks they are smart enough to give us wisdom. He should know.
2. The fact that ants can teach us—is humbling.

Some lessons

- Ants can lift twenty times their body weight (some say 100 times). They work all day, with all their might. Lesson: We might be able to leverage and accomplish a lot more than we think we can.
- Ants work as a team. How many times have you seen them work in long lines, moving food, or building a hill? Have you seen an ant find something too large to move and then a team would line up to move the object? Lesson: Without a team the dream dies and without a dream the team (colony) dies. John Maxwell might have said that. That sounds like something he would say. I certainly have never had an original thought that good.
- Ants know they shouldn't eat all the bread. Ants have a dream, God says, to store up for the winter. They don't eat all they carry home. They save and plan. They know tough days are coming. Lesson: Stop eating all you get.
- Common goals should pull people together like the awareness of "difficult winter days ahead." If ants "pull together," we should too. Lesson: Get over your differences with yourself and others, and work as a team.
- As with Tamerlane's ant, ants don't quit until they win. I have sprayed, stomped, wiped up, knocked off, powdered, pelted, and

pounced on ants. Not one of those methods was effective. When ants want food for the colony to survive, we can completely exhaust ourselves trying to stop them. They understand Tenacity. They keep coming and conquering. Ants keep the Target in mind. Lesson: Be like the ants and don't stop until you reach the Target you have set. Perseverance is the Trick. As with Tamerlane, there will be times when the "team" gets beat (momentarily). Don't fix the blame (adding shame) and point fingers when you meet with your team. Fix the problem and get going.

• When I was a teenager, I enjoyed making cookies. I only knew one recipe and actually that is still all I know (the recipe is on the website: 21-Ts.com).

One day I decided to enjoy a batch. Quick—easy—and delicious. I gathered *all the ingredients* and placed them on the counter. I placed the milk, sugar, cocoa, and other ingredients in a pan. To bring them to a boil takes a few minutes and then the ingredients boil hard for one minute. While I was busy, ants discovered the peanut butter I left open on the counter. When the boiling mixture was ready for the peanut butter, I discovered the jar was crawling, quit literally, with ants. I looked for another jar of peanut butter, but this process is fast. In seconds, the boiling ingredients would be hardening in the pan and I could not find another jar. The peanut butter's moment was now. I looked at the pot of steaming ingredients and the ants swarming in my peanut butter. What was I going to do? The one-minute timer was buzzing.

I was not going to waste the cookies. I mixed in the ants, scooped out the desired amount of peanut butter, and threw it into the steaming mixture. The lesson: Ants add a little crunch to no-bake oatmeal cookies.

Today, after I (supposedly had) finished this chapter, my wife and I went for a walk. As we find in South Carolina at this time of year, ants build hills everywhere. As we walked, we stepped on a hill and ants went scurrying. By the Time we returned, they were moving the eggs below the surface again and rebuilding their home. They did not allow a being 1,000 times taller (and I won't go into how much heavier) to stop them.

Start right *here*, in whatever "corn crib" you find yourself—with the troops dispersed, or the ants infesting your peanut butter—and get up. Then get moving in the direction of your Targets and goals. Keep pulling your piece of corn, even if it takes seventy, eighty or ninety tries to go from *here* to *there*. Be an example of Tenacity!

A SIMPLE OBSERVATION:

There's a lot of wisdom in an ant.
In a word—Tenacity!

THINGS TO THINK THROUGH:

- ◆ Do you give up at the first setback or sore muscles?
- ◆ Do you realize most winners win with bruises? Think about this. When an NFL game ends, do you think players on both teams might need some bandages and casts occasionally? Are you willing to work-on when you hurt?
- ◆ To you, are setbacks and delays reasons to quit, or a reason to dig in?
- ◆ Did you notice in the long list of quotes I shared, that throughout the ages, from every continent, people have learned Tenacity is a very valuable Trick? Is Tenacity one of your Tools for Transformation?
- ◆ If Tenacity is not currently included in your Toolbox of Tricks, who can show you how to develop it?

ANCIENT WRITINGS: "Take a lesson from the ants, you lazy fellow. Learn from their ways and be wise! For though they have no king to make them work, yet they labor hard all summer, gathering food for the winter. But you—all you do is sleep. When will you wake up? 'Let me sleep a little longer!' Sure, just a little more! And as you sleep, poverty creeps upon you like a robber and destroys you; want attacks you in full armor."

BOOKS: *The Go Getter* by Peter B. Kyne
Endurance: Shackletons' Incredible Voyage by Alfred Lansing
The Little Red Hen or *The Tortoise and the Hare* by Aesop
Total Money Makeover by Dave Ramsey

MOVIE: *42* about the legendary Jackie Robinson

I WILL APPLY THIS PRINCIPLE BY:_____

_____

_____

_____

I need a Teacher to help me move from here to there. When I have a Target, the proper Teacher will naturally Transmit the Terms and appropriate Technique(s) to me. When accompanied with Trust, this Training will influence my Thoughts and help me understand the Tools and Technology, along with the Tricks of the *Trade* . . .

CHAPTER L

Trade

D r. Ben Kulp is a dentist in Spartanburg, SC. As I interviewed him about his potential service on the Carolina Pregnancy Center board, I asked, "Mr. Kulp, if you decide to serve on this board, what activity are you going to say no to?" He looked at me rather puzzled and I said, "Sir, you are filling twenty-four hours a day with family, work, and church responsibilities. If you serve on the board, we expect you to invest four to six hours a month on projects to advance the center."

It occurred to me in that moment that we all are constantly saying yes and no. If Ben currently spent Saturday evening boating, napping, or mowing the yard, he would have to deny himself that (or other personal time) to make room to serve. Somewhere, he was going to have to say no to say yes. He had to Trade something here if he wanted to go There.

Applying this Principle in Life

Daniel Greene is a businessman from Greenville, SC, or should I say, Lake Keowee. He is the poster child for understanding the power of saying no when it comes to Trading.

Several years ago he bought a business doing about $800,000 a year. He told many of the original customers no, in a nice way. On the wall, he placed a sign which read: "$50.00 Minimum Order." Then he found new customers who needed $5,000.00 jobs produced. He diligently built that company to over $8,000,000 a year. Daniel and his wife Stacy sold the business (in their 40s) and are enjoying semi-retirement on Lake Keowee.

When we constantly say yes to the status quo, we will always stay right *here* at $800,000 a year. At some point we must say no so we can move on and begin Trading for different results.

Who Changes the World?

Transformation requires your involvement, so let's actually engage in this experiment now. I will provide you with the first three names and you can list the other seven people who have changed the world in your opinion.

Your answers don't have to be presidents or world renowned individuals. They could be simple people who made an impact in their world. It could be someone who changed the life of a child in your community.

1. Abraham Lincoln
2. Martin Luther King Jr.
3. Emma Fugate (an elderly neighbor)
4.
5.
6.
7.
8.
9.
10.

What do you think was the common denominator in each person's ability to impact the world around them?

- Age?
- Race?
- Sex?

- Physical appearance?
- Field of expertise?
- His or her time in history?

If your list is like mine, the list contains various ages, sexes, races, and occupations. However, there is more than likely one common denominator. I would guess the reason they made your list is they influenced the world through their chosen Trade (work or occupation). Mrs. Fugate was a neighbor who became a grandma to me. I visited her often and listened to her play the piano.

What you Trade your Thoughts, Time, and energy for will determine the major contributions of your life and destiny.

What Are You Trading Your Life For?

Do you remember Bobby (Chapter J Technology)? He manages the technicians in the heating business. You may recall he had earned a computer programming degree, did four years of military service, and returned home with an obsolete degree.

Bobby was in a registration line at a community college after he was discharged from the military. He asked the receptionist what degrees were available. At that moment the heating and air professor passed by and she suggested talking to him. He did and has been in the heating business for thirty years. Influences can come unexpectedly. Once Bobby decided to spend Time with the Teacher, he found his path in life. As you begin your process of picking your Teachers, learning the Terms, accepting the Transmission, and learning the Techniques, then the process has already begun.

Trade, with all of its varied definitions, is a process of exchanging one thing for another. Are you making the correct Trades in your life? If not, how will you change your decision making process?

Let's look at the alphabet.

ABCDEFGHIJKLMNOPQRSTUVWXYZ

In the many instances in which you rhymed or sang the alphabet, have you ever noticed that the designers might have wanted us to understand two words? The alphabet Teaches us to be friendly and Trade wisely.

ABCDEFG**HI**JKLM**NO**PQRSTUVWXYZ

There you have the first consideration in Trading. "Hi, thanks for asking. But no thank you." You can spend your Time, energy, and money on a million different ideas, projects, and jobs. To hit *the* goal *you* have set, *you* must constantly say no to everything that can sidetrack you.

Mary Lou Retton was an Olympian of unusual excellence. In an interview she said that once she set her Target/goal to become an Olympian, dates, proms, and all extracurricular activities were unacceptable. She constantly told everyone she was unwilling to Trade her life for something other than her goal. That decision not only took her to her goal, it took her to the *gold*. Go to http://marylouretton.com/ML_utube.html to watch the moment Click on Albums and then Olympic moments.

Saying No Will Save You Time

I am not sure what you will have to say no to. I don't know what your big yes is either. But I know this—you don't have to have a goal and you don't need discipline. You can say yes to everyone and everything and be nothing and do nothing. The issue is this: What do you want bad enough to tell everything else, *no?*

Mom just called. I have to run. I am saying no to writing so I can pick up my dad. I am back (forty-five minutes later). Dad is ninety-three, Mom is eighty-nine. We moved them in next door to "parent our parents." He fell—again—a few minutes ago. He didn't break any bones, thankfully. But I had to say no to this chapter to accomplish something much more valuable for the past few minutes. What are you Trading your resources for? Are you Trading for things others may see as important and missing the *real* goals you desire to reach?

Consider Saying No To:
- People and habits which hold you back.
- Things which keep you from your goals (petty ideas and small plans).
- Anything which would jeopardize your mind, body, or soul (a simple no in the back seat of a car could have saved many a girl an undesired pregnancy or, better yet, it could have kept them out of the back seat in the first place).
- Fights and information where there is no reward.
- Anything in which you won't be proud of the outcome.

Saying no to these items will help free your mind and spirit to say yes to your dreams, goals, and desired future . . . so your faith, family, freedom, and finances can flow.

A SIMPLE OBSERVATION:
Ralph Waldo Emerson said,
"Nothing great was ever achieved
without great enthusiasm."
Consider saying, "No" to thoughts and activities which
don't bring a harvest of right living and peace.

THINGS TO THINK THROUGH:
- What one habit in your life do you need to say no to?
- Are you Trading your life for the things you value most? If not, when will you start Trading differently?
- Zig Ziglar asked at a seminar I attended, "Do you believe there is any attitude or action you could change to make your life worse?" Is the opposite true? When will you start telling that bad action or habit no?
- Do you recall a Time when you really wanted to say no but said yes and ended up regretting it? How will you avoid the same blunder next Time?
- Are you enthusiastic about what you Traded your life for today?

ANCIENT WRITINGS: "The man who had received the five talents went at once and put his money to work and gained five more."

BOOKS: *The Go Getter* by Peter B. Kyne
The Strangest Secret by Earl Nightingale (Published by Simple Truths)

I WILL APPLY THIS PRINCIPLE BY:_____

_____

_____

_____

I need a Teacher to help me move from here to there. When I have a Target, the proper Teacher will naturally Transmit the Terms and appropriate Technique(s) to me. When accompanied with Trust, this Training will influence my Thoughts and help me understand the Tools and Technology, along with the Tricks of the Trade. If the teacher lives *Truth (or not)* . . .

CHAPTER M

Truth (Or Not)

A barber sees a boy passing his shop. With a mischievous grin, he walks towards the door saying, "Watch this."

"Excuse me, young man. Would you stop in for a minute?" The boy enters as the barber returns to the chair. "This is the dumbest kid in town," he whispers to his customer. "I can prove it to you."

The customer's eyes grow wide.

The boy asks with great enthusiasm. "How can I help you, sir?"

The barber extends his hands with a dollar bill in one and a five in the other.

The barber asks, "Which do you want?"

The boy takes the dollar, thanks the barber, and hurries out.

The barber roars with laughter. "That kid never learns. What did I tell you? That is the dumbest boy in town."

Soon the customer leaves. As he exits he sees the boy and calls, "Excuse me. May I ask you a question?"

"How could I help you?" the boy replies, licking his ice cream.

"Why did you take the dollar?"

The boy enjoys another lick on his cone, obviously enjoying the moment. He smiles and replies, "The day I take the five, this game is over!"

What Is the Truth?

It was the second day of the convention. 10,000 plus teenagers were gathered on the campus of the University of Illinois for a youth conference. The theater-style seating, the soft fabric and contour, brought extra weight to my already heavy eyelids during the afternoon session. The speaker was a sociology professor from Philadelphia, Dr. Anthony Campolo. He was talking about what real success involves. Somewhere in my sleepy condition I heard him say that while we struggle to pay for that new car, forty thousand people a day are starving to death.

I was thinking: *That is terrible.*

Dr. Campolo repeated, "Do you understand? Forty thousand people a day starve!"

That is really terrible.

There was a long pause (or maybe I went back to sleep).

His tone was thunderous and his message shocking as he projected his main point. "Forty thousand people a day starve, but you don't give a s_ _ _."

What did he say? I was now fully awake.

Then he brought the speech to a close. "But the real problem is . . . you care more that I said 's_ _ _' than you do about the 40,000 people who are starving every day."

The dictionary does not determine which words are important or which words carry value. Our Teachers and our hearts do that as we place value on different words and discover Truth. The Truth that day for me was . . . Dr. Campolo was right. I cared more about the word s_ _ _ than the forty thousand people. My values changed. His words caused my understanding of Truth to be altered.

Being True—In Words

A king was about to give the executioner a signal to pull the cord, allowing the floor to drop so the criminal would die by hanging. However, before the signal, the king asked the criminal if he had a final wish. He asked for a glass of water. The king obliged. Once the water was delivered, the criminal's hands began to shake. The king said, "Sir, take your Time, you will not be hung until you finish drinking the entire glass of water."

The criminal threw the water to the ground. The king said, "Release him. My word is true."

Being True—In Actions

The Greeks loved the theater. Their actors and actresses wore masks. Those individuals acquired a name, from which we get our English word "hypocrite" (to wear a mask). We can all have them. If we are not careful, when we walk into a new environment, the mask can go on. But in our hearts we know we are hiding. If you and your Teacher are not careful, you will both wear masks. Don't act as though you understand when you don't. That is wearing a mask.

Would you rather be respected for who you are or honored for who you are not? Start doing what you said you will do, when you said you will do it, as it should be done, and you will be living according to (your) Truth.

Being True—In Our Belief about Values

My oldest son Tucker likes to tell a joke about King James. It goes like this. When the King James 1611 translation of the Bible was finished, the king himself was impressed, but also concerned. He summoned a translator. "This is outstanding work. But sir, I have noted that in Exodus, chapter 20 and division 14 you have added an unnecessary three-letter word. In your next edition, please remove the three-letter word."

With a perplexed look, the esteemed scholar hurried to discover the nature of the error. He quickly found the passage and read, "Thou shalt *not* commit adultery."

Could ever-so-slight *mistakes* regarding truth alter our destiny? Is your Teacher leading you from a position of Truth? How do you know?

Following a Teacher, learning Terms, and using Tools in an improper way will yield Transformation, but *not* the one you might desire. We will absorb, receive, and learn what the Teacher is Transmitting—no matter the value, accuracy, or Truth found in the Teacher's message or life.

Sam Wyche is a former professional football player turned business man and sportscaster. He told me, "Never give a command that can be understood. Only give commands that cannot be misunderstood." Sam attributed this quote to General Douglas MacArthur. The Truth must be clearly spoken in a war situation because life and death hang in the balance. It is the same in our lives. What we accept as Truth will effect everything.

Being True—in Our Belief about Eternity

Every society has forms of worship. They intuitively know there is more to this life than a physical existence.

Dr. Roger McKenzie, Religion Professor at Southern Wesleyan University, says there are a few exceptions, such as a group known as the Sadducees, but most religions have some type of afterlife teaching. It is universally accepted there is something-out-there after death.

I desire to stay true to my word regarding the purpose of the book. It is not designed to tell you which road to take or which teachers to pursue. But I do want to give you options and things to consider throughout.

In some areas Truth is non-negotiable. There is not a surgeon in the world who will tell you to leave a ruptured appendix unattended. Death is eminent. It has to go. Firemen do not leave people trapped in cars which are smoldering. They cut them out.

One man said, "I am the way, and the truth, and the life." That is rather intolerant. An early follower had preformed a miracle using His authority and said, "I'll be completely frank with you—we have nothing to hide. By the name of Jesus Christ of Nazareth, the One you killed on a cross, the One God raised from the dead, by means of his name this man stands before you healthy and whole . . . salvation comes no other way; no other name has been or will be given to us by which we can be saved, only this one."

"I am the Truth—no other name—no other way." That sounds totally intolerant to me. Actually, it is narrow. Is Truth that narrow, *if* it is Truth?

I do not think Muslims, Jews, Christians, and Hindus (and many other groups) are wrong about the eternal aspect of life. They all agree there is an afterlife. Whatever you decide to worship or serve, make sure your god is a God who can create and sustain life and will ultimately hold you accountable. A God like that will give the best to you, and get the best thoughts, intentions, and actions out of you.

If the foundation of your life is Terms, and I believe that to be true, then Truth is the cement which holds those Terms together. What Truths are going to hold your life and dreams together? Do you want to build on sandy foundations which change, or on *the* Truth which never changes?

A SIMPLE OBSERVATION:
"One problem with the Internet is—you can't tell if the sources are telling the Truth." – Abraham Lincoln

THINGS TO THINK THROUGH:
- An error as small as the word "not" can change a lot. Is there anything you have left out of your "Truth"?
- Could thinking the "dollar boy" is the lunatic make you one? Who understood the Truth?
- If we stay on the same course, could an error in our thinking cause us to miss our—*there*?
- Is pain your friend? Read the book mentioned below to discover Truth about pain. *
- What question(s) do you need to ask yourself?
- Go to 21-Ts.com to continue studying Truth.

ANCIENT WRITINGS: "Jesus answered, 'I am the way and the Truth and the life.'"

BOOK: * *The Gift Nobody Wants* by Paul Brand and Phillip Yancey

I WILL APPLY THIS PRINCIPLE BY:_____
_____
_____
_____

I need a Teacher to help me move from here to there. When I have a Target, the proper Teacher will naturally Transmit the Terms and appropriate Technique(s) to me. When accompanied with Trust, this Training will influence my Thoughts and help me understand the Tools and Technology, along with the Tricks of the Trade. If the teacher lives Truth (or not) and allows *Trips*, it will help . . .

CHAPTER N

Trips

While we are in school, most Teachers expect us to get "it" right 70% of the Time to pass. In the real world, in some Trades, 30% right will make you a millionaire. A person with a batting average of 300 in the major leagues will make a fortune. But a 300 batting average means the player got on base three out of ten times at bat. Or he "failed" 70% of the time.

As we reconsider the process of selecting a good Teacher, I want us to focus on another character trait they need—an attribute our Teacher must have as they continue to Train and Transform us. Remember, the Transformation should move smoothly, just as we learned to speak our native tongue naturally.

For my own personal use, I like the word Mistakes better than Trips, but since it does not start with T, I will use Trip. The Teacher must allow you to Trip *(make mistakes)* with permission.

Why? Because *all* of us make mistakes and *all success* is built on failure.

During a Q & A with a panel of Dan Kennedy's Platinum Mastermind members, Dr. Tom Orent gave a great piece of advice. In fact, it was his answer when Dan asked, "What is your best piece of advice?" Dr. Orent said, "Fall forward faster, because the people who have failed the most are the most successful."

Mistakes are inevitable when you pursue the life you desire. Don't be afraid to make mistakes and Trip. TV personality and comedian Bill Cosby used this line, "In order to succeed, your desire for success should be greater than your fear of failure." Bill Cosby Tripped, overcame, and is a success.

Consider These Book Titles and Themes

Failing Forward by John Maxwell, leadership guru, talks about people being blessed and "lucky," having the Midas Touch as the reason for their success. What is the real reason for their success? Is it family background, wealth, greater opportunities, high morals, an easy childhood? Maxwell says, "The difference between average people and achieving people is their perception of and response to failure" (*Trips*).

Famous Failures by Joey Green is described on Amazon as, "Hundreds of hot shots who got rejected, flunked out, worked lousy jobs, goofed up, or did time in jail before achieving phenomenal success."

The Power of Failure: 27 Ways to Turn Life's Setbacks Into Success is written by Charles C. Manz. Look at some of the chapter titles:

- To Succeed More, Fail More.
- Be a Successful Learner by Learning from Failures.
- Recognize Failure as the Lifeblood of Success.

From the preface: "I truly believe that I owe most of the success I have enjoyed to my willingness to fail, fail repeatedly, and fail well. That is really why I am writing this book: to give failure the credit it deserves and to hopefully help others discover the rich rewards it offers when it is handled wisely."

Tripping successfully is a skill you must learn. I am not sorry but rather excited to tell you that the Transition from *here* to *there* a process of: try-fail-adjust; try-fail-adjust; try-fail-adjust; try-fail-adjust; and then you try-fail-adjust again. Oh, then you try-fail-adjust again and again and again. Sometimes we trip sixty-nine times . . . or more. Keep getting up and trying again.

Go Back to the Beginning

Everything we have ever *mastered*, we learned through that same process—but we did more of it—try-fail-adjust multiple hundreds of times. When we were learning to speak, we said, "DaMeee," and everyone cheered. "Did you hear that? He said, 'Grandma.'" It was no more Grandma than Maui, but we tried. We continued to try, constantly adjusting our tones and enunciation with lots of failures until the word Grandma was repeated with accuracy . . . then NO one cheered.

A Poem to Consider

See It Through

When you're up against a trouble,
Meet it squarely, face-to-face;
Lift your chin and set your shoulders,
Plant your feet and take a brace.
When it's vain to try to dodge it,
Do the best that you can do;
You may fail, but you may conquer,
See it through!

Black may be the clouds about you
And your future may seem grim,
But don't let your nerve desert you;
Keep yourself in fighting trim.
If the worse is bound to happen,
Spite of all that you can do,
Running from it will not save you,
See it through!

Even hope may seem but futile,
When with troubles you're beset,
But remember you are facing

Just what other men have met.
You may fail, but fail still fighting;
Don't give up, whate'er you do;
Eyes front, head high to the finish.
See it through!

Edgar Guest

Consider These Examples

- 3M started in 1904 with sandpaper, selling $2,500 a month. Great start, but they were spending $9,000 a month.
- Fred Smith, who dreamed of FedEx, got a C on the paper in college that described the business.
- Oprah Winfrey, who knows a *little* about success said, "I don't believe in failure. It's not failure if you enjoy the process."

Oprah learned to fail successfully. Relax. You don't have to get it right all the time and certainly not the first time.

- Og Mandino is my favorite author. Let's look at some of his thoughts on failure.
  - Each failure to sell will increase your chances for success at your next attempt.
  - Failure will never overtake me if my determination to succeed is strong enough.

My son Tucker's screen saver says *FAIL BIG!* He hasn't had to study failure. He just had to be in the same room with me. I have failed a lot so he could pick it up naturally—just like he learned English. Most people don't prepare and are not taught to deal with failure. Do you have a Teacher/mentor who can Teach you to Trip (make mistakes) well? If you will look at most Teachers' pencils, you will note they use their eraser too. Albert Einstein, one of the greatest minds of the last century said, "Anyone who never made a mistake has never tried anything new."

Consider These People

He started in his home garage. His very first venture went bankrupt. During his first press conference, a newspaper editor ridiculed him because he had no good ideas. (Walter Disney)

His first novel was rejected by sixteen agents and twelve publishing houses. The media now calls him one of the best fiction authors alive. (John Grisham)

You ever heard of a Sony electric rice cooker? Actually it was a burner. They only sold 100 of these "burners." Today, Sony is the world's 6th largest electronic company. (Akio Morita)

Are you willing to view your Trips as steps to success and get up and keep moving forward?

A SIMPLE OBSERVATION:

Considered the greatest basketball player of all time by many people, Michael Jordan said, "I have failed over and over and over again in my life. And that is why I succeed."

THINGS TO THINK THROUGH:

- If you decide today to start a new career, are you willing to go *through* the failures to reach your goal?
- Are your Teachers allowing you to fail without condemnation and shame?
- Do you overly concern yourself that your ideas may fail? Consider Robert Townsend. He masterminded the Avis car rental company turnaround. He said that two of every three decisions he made were wrong. Can you relax, try, fail, and adjust?
- Could fear of failure be keeping you from stretching towards your dreams?
- Hilton Johnson says, "Achieving a goal is not as rewarding as overcoming the failures that got you there." Do you think that is true? Why or why not?

ANCIENT WRITINGS: "Don't you know that this good man, though you trip him up seven times, will each time rise again? But one calamity is enough to lay you low."

BOOK: *Psycho Cybernetics* by Maxwell Maltz, M.D.

I WILL APPLY THIS PRINCIPLE BY:_____

_____

_____

_____

I need a Teacher to help me move from here to there. When I have a Target, the proper Teacher will naturally Transmit the Terms and appropriate Technique(s) to me. When accompanied with Trust, this Training will influence my Thoughts and help me understand the Tools and Technology, along with the Tricks of the Trade. If the teacher lives Truth (or not) and allows Trips, it will help. Over *Time* ...

CHAPTER O

Time

She had been a full-time homemaker and mother for over forty years. But this was also her first speech—ever.

The speaker and the audience were both engaging slowly. She was testing the audience like you might put your foot into the water before jumping in. They could tell the speaker was nervous by her white knuckles on the podium. But it did not take long for the speaker to know the temperature was okay, and she "jumped in" with both feet.

> Ladies, I know what it is like to work. For several years my husband was homebound after a crane dropped a piece of steel and crushed his leg. There were times when I would wash, clean, and cook for nine people on a daily basis.
>
> One morning I was busy vacuuming. I heard a rather noticeable knock at the door. I answered it. All smiles, a young man was selling brushes. He described in detail his box of wares. After his enthusiastic sales pitch, I made a purchase. Politely thanking me, my salesman, who must have been five (my youngest child) ran off. I returned to the vacuuming—my heart singing.

A few years later, I recall sitting before a pile of clothes. My son ran into the room, "Mom, you must come." I left the laundry. He took me to a tree and began searching. "Look there!" he exclaimed. I saw it—an inchworm. We watched the little "fella" make his way across a leaf. After several minutes of "Look, he's stretching . . . he has a string . . . look at how green he is," my little scientist had exhausted his research and was ready for a different adventure. He thanked me and ran off. I returned to folding clothes, still smiling from the moment of excitement and education.

The years passed and our nest was becoming . . . not empty, but . . . spacious. At seventeen he, as always, ran into the house, "Mom, I have an hour; let's sling some mud!" That is code for, "Let's go 4-wheelin." I was elbow deep in dishwater. Nevertheless, I left and for the next hour, I had the ride of my life. We took "Hilde," his old Bronco—as he affectionately called her—and headed to the woods. We made our own road through the creek, over rocks, and to the top of a mountain.

Ladies, what a view! That was an adventure that I am certainly glad I experienced. He dropped me off and headed back to work. I entered our "spacious" home, returned to the dishes, and stored another memory.

Having floors to vacuum, laundry to fold, and dishes to do is common. It is a necessary part of our lives whether we are newly married, raising children, or—like my dear Edsel and me—alone, puttering around an empty house, listening to silence and the tick-tock of passing time.

If you are fortunate enough to still have opportunities, listen for the knocks. Leave the common chores and fling open the door of your house and heart. Inspire your salesman or scientist with your lavish investment of love and *Time*. Those dishes will be there long after your 4-wheeler has grown and gone.

I guess these days Edsel and I are looking backward as

much as we do forward. I am still vacuuming . . . I am still folding clothes . . . I am still doing dishes. The difference is . . . today . . . nobody's knocking.

There was silence in the room. I am not sure the speaker knew which way to go. She spoke slowly.

Ladies, I am proud to return this podium to my salesman, scientist, and 4-wheel enthusiast, who now happens to be your pastor.

The Power of Love - Shown By Time

The consistent love of a Trusted Teacher or parent does many things to the mind and soul of a child. It removes self-doubt, like the constant dripping of water removes the rock. "Water is fluid, soft, and yielding. But water will wear away rock, which is rigid and cannot yield. As a rule, whatever is fluid, soft, and yielding will overcome whatever is rigid and hard. This is another paradox: what is soft is strong" (Lao-Tzu). Love spelled TIME can soften a hardened attitude.

If an adult will give a child Time, it answers a lot of other questions. Are my questions okay? Am I worth anything? When someone invests their Time in us, our rough edges, self-doubts, and fears can be washed away. I learned to sell at that door where a mom always gave me her Time and always made a purchase.

"He who stays flexible—never gets bent out of shape," is the way my wife says it. Mom was flexible. She did not get bent out of shape (much). Her willingness to yield molded me. Is your Teacher/mentor willing to give freely of their Time to help you in your Transition from *here* to *there*?

Time is Valuable (Priceless), Spend with Care

What we do with our Time really demonstrates our values. Much like the way we spend money, we only get one opportunity. Spending your money on a video game is not a problem as long as you don't want a motorcycle next week—to find the money was spent on a lesser goal, missing the greater opportunity. Spending your Time on a video game or watching TV when you could have been reading (like Ben Carson), will find you reaping different results tomorrow. The return will be extremely different. The opportunity is gone.

My sense of self-worth was created from a Teacher-mother who had Time for my experiments and sales calls. Make Time for what you cherish. There is no other way to give that person or project value.

Why would we include a story of a mother spending Time with her son in a book regarding Transformation? Let me offer a few reasons:

- To be real honest, I like this story. That was my mom.
- The best education and Transformation of our minds and spirits takes place naturally, as on a mother's knee. Many of us have heard someone say, "I worked with Mr. Braisted for nine months and learned more about (whatever) than I gained in four years of college." This will consistently be true. Ah-choo. Someone was taking time to personally sneeze on them.
- Some day the opportunities you have today, the knocks on your door, may pass. I shared this story to ask you: What will you regret tomorrow if you don't answer the knock today?

Time, the Great Equalizer

What do Michael Jordon, Michel Angelo, and Michael Dell all have in common? The name? Yes. But they all have twenty-four hours, just like you. They all choose how to spend their Time and what to give themselves to, just like you. The result? The life they have and the life you have.

Dealing with Time Past

I am grateful for my parents, but they failed in many areas. I wrestled for four years and Dad never showed up for one match. My dad never took me hunting, I always went alone. There are many things like that which must be forgiven and moved past. Make the choice to be "bigger than." Past regrets can infect today's special moments and sour tomorrow's dreams. My dad is one person I had to forgive and release

Dr. Les Parrott's words are being recalled from a speech he gave over twenty years ago. He had been wronged by some people. He went to his boss and asked what he should do about it. After explaining the situation, the overseer asked Les if the people came to him and asked for forgiveness would he forgive them? Les assured him that he would. His boss said, "Les, why don't you go ahead and forgive them anyway. That way if they ever ask you to forgive them you can say you already did. And if they never come and ask you, it won't make any difference, because you already did."

Now that you are at an age and a level of maturity where you can choose, find mentors who will "infect" you with the right values, spirit, and habits. If Les Parrot had sought counsel from someone who said, "Hold a grudge—get even," the man's future could have been extremely different.

While I am trying to finish the last of this chapter, I have a little girl named Sarah standing here. She says she will wait. But the swing in my backyard broke and she wants me to fix it. I just took her picture with an S-hook that we need to fix the swing. To her, the swing is the most important thing in the world. To me, right now, this book is. But in order to build a little girl's self-esteem and fix her crisis, I will be back. The knock may not return.

Are you looking to people to provide direction and influence in your life who are not wholesome? Some parents and caregivers were not wholesome role models. Some did not give you the Time you should have received. Everyone came from a biological flesh and blood mother. Some of you were fortunate to have a mother who valued you and spent Time with you. Others did not. Some reading this book were adopted. What a privilege for so many, and then for others, not so much. Either way, without that person, you would not have survived. Thank them. (More on Thanksgiving in Chapter R.) But don't let anything in your past keep you from your desired future. Forgive them and move on.

Seasons Are Important To Progress

We move through seasons, but we live in moments. If you can master the moment, you will understand Time. Don't let the season mess you up. Maybe you are in a fall or winter season and the branches look bare and not productive. Understand the season and keep working through it. A new season will come if you will stay in the moment until this season passes.

Your greatest gift is your Time

A SIMPLE OBSERVATION:
Vacuuming, laundry, and dishes—they need to be done,
but you better catch that son-on-the-run.

THINGS TO THINK THROUGH:
- Who has been your greatest mentor or person of influence in your life? Was time a factor in the power of that influence?
- You only get to spend your Time . . . once. What do you do where you lose the sense of Time?
- If you could change anything about how you have spent Time in the past, what would that be?
- Since you can't change a thing about yesterday—only learn and grow from it—how will you adjust, take responsibility, and make the best of whatever your past was filled with?
- Who should you give some time to – Right Now?

ANCIENT WRITINGS: "There is a Time for everything, and a season for every activity under heaven: a Time to be born and a Time to die, a Time to plant and a Time to uproot, a Time to kill and a Time to heal, a Time to tear down and a Time to build, a Time to weep and a Time to laugh, a Time to mourn and a Time to dance, a Time to scatter stones and a Time to gather them, a Time to embrace and a Time to refrain, a Time to search and a Time to give up, a Time to keep and a Time to throw away, a Time to tear and a Time to mend, a Time to be silent and a Time to speak, a Time to love and a Time to hate, a Time for war and a Time for peace."

BOOK: *First Things First* by Stephen R. Covey

I WILL APPLY THIS PRINCIPLE BY:_____
_____
_____
_____

I need a Teacher to help me move from here to there. When I have a Target, the proper Teacher will naturally Transmit the Terms and appropriate Technique(s) to me. When accompanied with Trust, this Training will influence my Thoughts and help me understand the Tools and Technology, along with the Tricks of the Trade. If the teacher lives Truth (or not) and allows Trips, it will help. Over Time the process will *Transform* me . . .

CHAPTER P

Transform

It was a gorgeous morning. My wife and I were cutting small trees and clearing weeds from the dampened soil softened by the spring rains. We were *alone*, in the woods, on the most beautiful lot in the world. What else could I want? Maybe a sandwich.

This sandwich had been built with love and excellence. It had a quarter inch of ham, tomato slices about an eighth of an inch thick, lettuce, mustard, and just a little mayo. The bread was whole wheat; the onions and pickles were perfect.

I had brushed off a stump and taken a seat. But have you ever noticed that it is hard to get everything right in your environment, and when you do, it's even harder to keep it right? That day was no different.

While I was enjoying my sandwich, a bee decided he would too. As I shook him away, I had a feeling of discontent. As I started to take another bite, my *friend*—or should I say my *thinking*—caused another feeling. But this Time the feeling was intensifying.

With greater emotion, the bee was thrown from my sandwich, (along with the tomato). My feelings changed, but not for the good. Before I could take another bite, he was back again. I took off my hat, stabilized my sandwich, and—POW. He fell and I felt a little better, for .008 seconds—

because he was back eating my sandwich in .0081 seconds. This time my sandwich looked like a sand*mush*—tomato missing and broken bread. However, I still wanted to *enjoy* it, without the bee.

For the second time, I took my hat and smacked the bee. The bee hit the ground.

Victory at last.

I only had a moment of triumph, then the fight started again. The bee came back and so did the feelings. I gripped my hat, placed my crumpled sand*mush* at just the right distance, and—BAMM! I sent him to the ground. But I did not stop there; I stood up and stepped on him, smashing him into that soft dirt.

My feeling changed a little, for the good.

As I tried to get my feelings and sand*mush* organized, a motion caught my eye. That bee was pushing himself up out of the earth. I could not believe it. I out-weighed him ten thousand to one, but he was fighting back. I said *things* went down, but I should have said, *I* went down—down to get a closer look.

He was appraising the situation. One wing had a hole; the other looked like a crumpled piece of paper. He began to rotate and shake his wings as though checking the bearings. He created spit, wax, honey (I don't know which), and began patching the hole. He would shake the wing dry, then spit, shake, and dry . . . spit, shake, and dry. He began to press his wing between his legs as you would iron a pair of pants.

By this time, I was almost touching him. Thirty seconds earlier I wanted to kill the pest and now, a totally different feeling. Now I was praying he would patch the holes and make it.

"I am sorry," I said out load. He continued to spit and iron that wing, filling in the holes. He continually repeated the process. At this point, the wing with a hole must have satisfied him (or her) and he placed attention on the crumpled wing. This wing was pressed between his legs. It reminded me of putting butter on a piece of toast, only he was buttering it on both sides at the same time. He shook it, applying the buttering strokes back and forth across the wing.

By this point, I had changed. I found myself excited for him. I am praying, encouraging, and cheering for my friend. "Come on. You can do it."

Finally, the bee seemed to be satisfied with his repairs and he flew away. Well, he took off. He only made it about three feet and crashed. Since I was kneeling, I crawled over to him. He continued working. Soon, he took flight and disappeared down the mountain.

All of a sudden I realized I was on my knees. I stayed there a long time. Did the place change? Did things change? No. Was my sand*mush* still ruined? Yes, but that bee Transmitted his passion to win and overcome anything that came against him. Watching him fight for survival, Transformed me. I had gone from hate to love in less than two minutes. A miracle—a Transformation—had taken place, both on wings and within me.

This story is true. I have long forgotten where I read it, but the original writer's Transformation became mine through the power of an illustration.

When I am tempted to cuss and kick a can, (as I am at times), I stop, remember that bee, and think, *There might be a miracle here if I would just slow down.*

A Process of Transformation

Transformation can take place instantly, but usually there is a transitioning to Transformation. We are not here and then instantly there. From wanting to learn English to mastering the language, there is usually Time, Trips, and Training until the Transition process is experienced.

Fred Smith, the owner of FEDEX, held up his arm at the conference in San Diego California. (His arm was in a sling or cast as I recall). He asked, "Is this a problem?" The attendees said, "Yes." He said, "No, this is a fact. How I think and what I do with it determines if it is a problem or not."

Situations vary, but people are much the same. We all have "things in slings," or "bees on sandwiches" which can be problems—or not. It depends on how we shape and Transform their image in our minds. For Fred Smith to see the sling as a fact, he had learned to process information differently. His thinking was Transformed. There are other people, like the attendees, who would tend to see the sling as a problem.

This Process will Work In You

This Transformation principle can be effective in all areas of your life because it takes place *in* you, *if* you apply it.

The Transformation you desire first begins in you, then through you, and, ultimately, around you. When you find yourself in a growing, transitioning mode, you will find yourself saying, "I have never done this before." New Terms, Techniques, Tricks, and exposure to new Teachers will take you through a Transition which will bring Transformation. Consider looking at those new "challenges" as facts, not problems.

Transformation can take place instantly too. Fred Smith also shared a story at that conference about preparing to go away for the weekend to rest. He came in from work and was sitting in a recliner, where he should have been relaxing. Instead he found himself irritated (*here*) that everything was not ready to go so he could relax (*there*). He had to re-visit his view of the beautiful, plush recliner he was in (but not enjoying).

There will be days the bee will land. Today, I have about forty-five minutes before I take some boys camping. Tired? Busy? Behind on a commitment? Phone calls to make? Yes. So I have a decision: Am I going to enjoy the Trip, or fret about 101 things? The bee has landed.

Repent is a great word for this process. It comes from two Latin words which mean to *return* and *think again*. When I returned to the bee and re-thought, I was Transformed.

Is there something bothering you? Are you afraid of something? If you don't chase it, it might chase you. By changing your point of view, slowing down, and rethinking, Transformation can take place. What do you need to re-think? Re-thinking can Transform you—positively of negatively. You can be enjoying the circumstances and start cussing, or you can be cussing and start enjoying—it will work either way. Your choice.

A SIMPLE OBSERVATION:

"There are only two ways to live your life. One is as though nothing is a miracle. The other is as though everything is a miracle."
— Albert Einstein

THINGS TO THINK THROUGH:

- What can you learn from the bee?
- When you have a potentially "stinging" situation in your life, do you destroy or cheer for the "bee"?
- You may have cussed many situations (bees), but you *decide* you want to change your approach. What will need to change in you?
- The bee was not deterred or defeated by size. How can you approach your challenges as he did?
- Do you have any situations which might be bothering you today that you would turn into a Transformational (miracle) moment?

ANCIENT WRITINGS: "But the seed on good soil stands for those with a noble and good heart, who hear the word, retain it, and by persevering produce a crop."

BOOK: *The Choice* by Og Mandino

I WILL APPLY THIS PRINCIPLE BY:_____

_____

_____

_____

I need a Teacher to help me move from here to there. When I have a Target, the proper Teacher will naturally Transmit the Terms and appropriate Technique(s) to me. When accompanied with Trust, this Training will influence my Thoughts and help me understand the Tools and Technology, along with the Tricks of the Trade. If the teacher lives Truth (or not) and allows Trips, it will help. Over Time the process will Transform me so I can *Teach* . . .

CHAPTER Q

Teach Others

Our youngest daughter has Down syndrome. Her name is Katelyn Amanda Joy (which means - pure loveable joy). She is ten but seldom makes it to the potty. She can feed herself if you get the food on the spoon. She can't talk, but she communicates tremendous love. I love her as only a "Daddy-0" can, but I don't seem to be able to Teach her very much. But she Teaches us—constantly—without a word.

When do you qualify to Teach others? You have been a Teacher from day one. I had never been a Daddy-0 before my son Tucker was born. He was Teaching me to be a dad from the moment we found out Kathy, my wife, was pregnant. Before birth, I prayed for him and his (now) wife, Jess. He was Teaching me to be a Daddy-0.

Even beyond passive teaching, suppose the Teacher in the first grade explains a math problem. Tucker understands, but his neighbor, Sally, does not understand. If Tucker can explain it in a way Sally comprehends, he has just mastered teaching at a new level, above that of the Teacher. We all Teach constantly.

Heading To College

Dr. Marlin Elliott, my favorite college professor, taught: "If you came to this college knowing everything, and leave knowing nothing, you have been educated." To look at this from Dr. Elliott's perspective, a Teacher is someone who understands how much *they* don't know and helps you understand how much *you* don't know. Dr. Elliott was the only non-*up-chuck* professor I had. As I progressed through college, it became apparent how to get good grades. Listen to and "eat" what the professor "feeds" you. Then on test day, *up-chuck* it (or throw it back up). If you could *throw-up* enough of what they fed, a good grade was your reward. (This is called *Banking*, I think, in educator's Terminology.)

Dr. Elliott was different. He wanted you to *think*. He wanted you to enlarge your understanding of yourself and others. He did not want you to know what he knew, but what you could discover—from him and from 10,000 other sources. Coach John Wooden said it this way, "It is what we learn after we think we know it all that really matters."

Your Ears—As a Teacher

A man said to the Teacher Socrates, so this age-old story has been told, "Do you know what I just heard about your friend?"

"Hold on a minute," Socrates replied. "Before telling me anything, I'd like to pass the information through a Test. It's called the 'Triple Filter Test.' The first filter is 'Truth.' Have you made absolutely sure that what you are about to tell me is true?"

"No," the man said. "Actually, I just heard about it and—"

"All right," said Socrates. "So you don't really know if it's true or not. Now, let's try the second filter, the filter of 'Goodness.' Is what you are about to tell me about my friend something good?"

"No, on the contrary," the man admitted.

Socrates clarified, "So, you want to tell me something bad about him, but you're not certain it's true? You may still pass; there's one filter left: the filter of 'Usefulness.' Is what you want to tell me about my friend going to be useful to me?"

"No, not really," the man admitted with head down.

"Well," concluded Socrates, "if what you want to tell me is neither true nor good nor useful, why tell it to me at all?"

So the story goes silent . . . which would be a great thing to happen to many conversations.

Your Study Habits

The last day of college, Dr. Elliott, *woke* me up with these words. "At the beginning of this semester, I assigned no collateral reading in this course. I challenged you to research, develop, and read where you were challenged related to this subject matter. In your syllabus there were many books, authors, and resources you could find to expand your thinking. That was your launching pad to discovery. I would like for you to give me the approximate number of pages you read in subject matter related to this class in the blank line at the bottom of the test."

Then, as I recall, he wrote these two words on the board.

Pedagogy   Andragogy

I did not have a clue what they meant or even how to say them. Under each he wrote a definition.

Methods used to teach a child   Methods used to teach adults

He explained the definitions and continued to explain their value to us. "When I Teach a child, I have to make requirements very clear. I have to give them step-by-step instructions. Objectives have to be plain."

"When I Teach an adult, I expect him or her to be able to find the Truth. I expect an adult to have personal incentive and be self-directed. They need to research, study, and struggle with the material, without someone having to look over their shoulder on a daily basis. The number of pages you listed on this sheet will be reflected in your grade. The grade you will get in life."

Dr. Elliott, as mentioned, was not a "throw-up" professor. He was a man who could read and write six (or seven) languages. He was brilliant, but he did not get there by being a child. He was an adult when it came to his study habits and teaching abilities. He could pass it on.

Do you want to know what I wrote on the blank line on that page? I hate to tell you—0.

Your Words As a Teacher

A Doctor James—from another generation—wrote these words.

> Don't be in any rush to become a Teacher, my friends. Teaching is highly responsible work. Teachers are held to the strictest standards. And none of us is perfectly qualified. We get it wrong nearly every time we open our mouths. If you could find someone whose speech was perfectly true, you'd have a perfect person, in perfect control of life.
>
> A bit in the mouth of a horse controls the whole horse. A small rudder on a huge ship in the hands of a skilled captain sets a course in the face of the strongest winds. A word out of your mouth may seem of no account, but it can accomplish nearly anything—or destroy it!
>
> It only takes a spark, remember, to set off a forest fire. A careless or wrongly placed word out of your mouth can do that. By our speech we can ruin the world, turn harmony to chaos, throw mud on a reputation, send the whole world up in smoke, and go up in smoke with it, smoke right from the pit of hell.
>
> This is scary: You can tame a tiger, but you can't tame a tongue—it's never been done. The tongue runs wild, a wanton killer.

The tongue has the power of life and death. Learn to talk less and listen more. How can we pick the right Teachers and then, in turn, Teach right? Consider the following.

Watch—What Comes Out of Your Mouth

I know that watching words is an impossibility in the physical—words are invisible. Or are they? "Sticks and stones may break my bones, but words will never hurt me." How much error can you pack in a sentence? The few times I have been hit with a stick, I have soon forgotten the damage. However, words have cut to the very core of my heart and I have carried some for years. I have seen the blessing and the damage words can have on one's life. Those who speak empowering, encouraging, and enthusiastic words give life. Sometimes those words are a rebuke or correction, but they contain power. Are you the kind of person that gives others energy? Or do you suck the life out of people around you with your words?

Pick friends and acquaintances that mutually encourage one another. Pick friends which never deliberately pull the other away from their highest goals and ideals. They will give life.

Teachers Are Students

If your Teachers were totally honest, they would all admit they are still in the student mode as they Teach. The Teacher is learning about Teaching while trying to Teach the student about Teaching. Teachers are constantly students. Students are constantly Teachers. Their pencil still has an eraser.

In *Success 101*, John Maxwell, business guru, identifies seven areas that successful people must self-manage:

- Your emotions
- Your time
- Your priorities
- Your energy
- Your thinking
- Your words
- Your personal life.

Your Teachers must *learn* to manage themselves first. They need to constantly learn and live these principles.

As Maxwell explains it, managing your words (tongue) is only one of the seven characteristics he lists. I wanted to add another T chapter—Tongue—but decided to bury it here. Wisdom is valued most when you dig for it. I hope we both will dig for this Truth with all our might.

As covered earlier, your words, Terms, and Thought processes determine the foundation of your life. But how does the tongue determine the direction of your life? Have you ever observed your nervous system as it relates to your tongue? It amazes me how the body responds to words. My stress, anger, and peace are affected by the words I speak. Many times, I will not get angry if I keep my mouth shut in a difficult situation.

The Terms and words you use will determine what you build with your life. The words determine if you get shoes or a ticket (Chapter H Thoughts). There is no need wondering what a group of teens were discussing before they robbed the convenience store. Their words determined their decision and destiny.

Children Teaching Children

The three Nalley children had Cystic Fibrosis. They were precious children and had much to Teach us through their short lives. Anthony, when he was four years old, observed a conversation between his father and his little sister Bethany.

George, the father, was explaining to Bethany the need to finish her cereal. Bethany, stubborn as a child can be, would not obey her father. George told her, "You do not have to eat it, now." George observed his children.

Anthony leaned over and told his sister, "Let me tell you from experience, it is better if you eat it *now*."

Teachers can come from any*where* at any*time*. The Pope and a Pauper are better than the Pope by himself.

Coach John Wooden won games consistently, but he started out as an English Teacher in Indiana. He understood the importance of words.

A SIMPLE OBSERVATION:
"Take the attitude of a student—never be too big to ask questions, never know too much to learn something new."

– Og Mandino

Life is Learning. Life is Teaching.

THINGS TO THINK THROUGH:

- In short, a Teacher is a salesman/saleswoman. They sell you their ideas as facts and foundations. Does your Teacher love to sell you what they know? (There is nothing wrong with this.)
- But, does your Teacher challenge you to grow beyond their own ability and knowledge base?
- Are you monitoring the words that come in? (Socrates)
- Are you monitoring what you meditate on?
- Are you thoughtful about the words that go out?

ANCIENT WRITINGS: "Pass on what you heard from me . . . to reliable leaders who are competent to teach others."

BOOK: *Teach With Your Strengths* by Rosanne Liesveld and Jo Ann Miller

I WILL APPLY THIS PRINCIPLE BY:_____
_____
_____
_____

I need a Teacher to help me move from here to there. When I have a Target, the proper Teacher will naturally Transmit the Terms and appropriate Technique(s) to me. When accompanied with Trust, this Training will influence my Thoughts and help me understand the Tools and Technology, along with the Tricks of the Trade. If the teacher lives Truth (or not) and allows Trips, it will help. Over Time the process will Transform me so I can Teach. If we continue to Trust and practice *Thanksgiving*, it will accelerate the Transformation . . .

CHAPTER R

Thanksgiving

An aging Quaker and his grandson sat on a bridge. They were relaxed, watching creation and listening to the gurgling stream below. They were enjoying the day together, while fishing and greeting neighbors and strangers alike.

Many of the conversations between grandfather and those passing seemed to be totally outside of the small boy's assessment. Grandpa would make small talk with old friends and occasionally be quite lengthy with others. However, as the day progressed, a few conversations began to puzzle the boy.

Hesitantly, the boy asked, "Grandpa, I am not quite sure how to ask this . . ."

Grandpa patiently encouraged his grandson to speak.

"I think you told someone a lie," the boy confided.

Grandpa, known as a man of highest integrity and truth, became very concerned. "What did I say?"

"A man with a cowboy hat mentioned he was considering moving to this area."

"Yes, I remember him from this morning; he worked with horses."

"That is the one. He asked you what kind of people lived in this town.

He also asked you what you thought about the possibility of building a strong and profitable business *here*. Then, you asked him what kind of people lived in the village from whence he came."

"I remember . . . continue, Son."

"You asked him if he had built a strong business *there?*"

"Yes, I recall," Grandpa stated.

"He told you that the village was full of crooks and unkind people. He said it was impossible to build a business *there*, and he did not appreciate the way people had treated him, which is why he left."

"Correct."

"I think you told him that the same kind of people he knew *there* lived *here*. You told him that he would find it tough to build a business *here*. You also told him we would not be thankful if he settled in this town."

"Yes, I recall that conversation. How did I lie?"

"I'm not sure yet, Grandpa." Searching for and finding the right words, the boy continued. "First, I don't know if people like that are in our town . . . but I thought you may know people that I do not know."

Grandpa nodded. "Okay, continue please. Is that where you thought I told a lie?"

"No," the boy said hesitantly, "a few minutes ago, another visitor asked almost the same questions. He wanted to resettle. He also wanted to know what kind of people lived *here* and what you thought his possibilities would be."

"Yes, and what did I ask him?" Grandpa questioned.

"You asked almost the same questions. What kind of business did you build where you were and what kind of people lived in that village?"

"What did the man answer?"

"The man said, 'Great, honest, and good people—who appreciated a quality product and were willing to pay a fair price for that kind of service.' He said some of the friendliest people in the world lived *there* and business could not be better. He had built a good business and was thankful for what he had been able to accomplish. He wanted to expand into other towns and give his business a chance to grow. That is when you looked straight at him and lied. You said 'Good and honest people lived here and he would be thankful he settled here, because his business would do well.'"

Brokenhearted, the grandson began to cry and asked, "How could a man who has taught me to always be honest, tell a lie? How could you tell one of those men something that was untrue?"

The thoughtful, wise old Quaker pulled his grandson close, kissed him on top of the head and whispered, "Thank you for sharing your uneasiness. I understand how you thought I lied. This may be hard to understand, but *both* answers are true. Son, in life, you not only *make* your environment, you actually carry it with you. Both men will naturally find exactly what they are, when they get *here*. If either chooses to settles *here*, they will find the same thing they found *there*. No matter where they go, both men will find that to be true, because they will bring it with them."

I want to tell you up front that I hope and pray this chapter becomes one of the most important Ts in this book for you. It might be *the* deciding factor if you enjoy your *here* while you travel through somewhere, on your way to *there*. And it will determine if you enjoy your *there* when you get *there*. It certainly will be an important ingredient in your happiness and success right *here*, and right now. This T provides its transforming power when you simply learn to say, "Thank You," because you are truly thank—full.

Wisdom Regarding Gratitude and a Good Attitude

"Gratitude is not only the greatest of all virtues, but the parent of all others." (Marcus Tullius Cicero, Roman statesman, lawyer, politician and philosopher)

Dr. Charles Swindoll has been the past president of Dallas Theological Seminary and has written more than seventy books, many best-sellers. He penned these words on attitude:

> The longer I live, the more I realize the impact of attitude on life. Attitude, to me, is more important than facts. It is more important than the past, than education, than money, than circumstances, than failures, than successes, than what other people think, say or do. It is more important than appearance, giftedness, or skill. It will make or break a company . . . a church . . . a home. The remarkable thing is we have a choice every day regarding

the attitude we embrace for that day. We cannot change our past . . . we cannot change the fact that people will act in a certain way. We cannot change the inevitable. The only thing we can do is play the one string we have, and that is our attitude. I am convinced that life is 10% what happens to me and 90% how I react to it. And so it is with you . . . we are in charge of our attitudes.

Country singer Willie Nelson understands the power of gratitude: "When I started counting my blessings, my whole life turned around."

"If the only prayer you say in your whole life is, "Thank you," that would suffice," said Meister Eckhart, the German theologian and philosopher.

Being Grateful in Unlikely Moments

Commentator Matthew Henry was robbed. He proceeded to tell some friends that he was Thankful. They were taken back and asked how a man could be grateful for having been robbed.

Matthew Henry gave his friends four reasons:

1. I have never been robbed before.
2. I was robbed of possessions but not life.
3. They took all I had, but I did not have much with me today.
4. Mainly, I am Thankful I was robbed and not the robber.

Living In the Here and Now

It is so, so easy to look back with anger and regret or forward in fear and doubt. Learning to live in the moment, abundant and free, is the way to true happiness and joy.

Since you take yourself everywhere you go . . . take a Thankful self. Until you are Thankful for who and what you are, what you have, who you are with, where you are, and where you are going, you will always be frustrated *here* and nothing will change when you reach *there*.

Most of the Ts that we are studying are things which must come to us—from without. This T is different. It is much like our Technique—Chapter

E—on Tenacity. You have a *here*—right now—to know, experience, and improve as you reach for your *there*. The question then becomes: How are you going to learn to appreciate your *here* so you will know how to appreciate your *there*?

One way, if not the best way, to improve your *here* is to practice the art of being Thankful. There are two ways to be wealthy. One is to be Thankful and content with what you have. The other is abundance. The problem is, you can have abundance, be very wealthy—have *everything*—but still be un-happy. No amount of fame, wealth, or any other created thing will be satisfactory without a Thankful heart.

A Letter from the SC Superintendent of Education

Dr. Zais is the Superintendent of Education for the State of South Carolina. When I asked him to evaluate a couple of chapters of this book, he wrote me regarding this very subject.

> Gene:
>
> I very much enjoyed reading what you have sent. I look forward to reading the completed book. One thing I learned from my father was to treasure the present moment. People spend so much time regretting the past and worrying about the future, that they fail to *appreciate* the now, the little joys of everyday living. The smell of coffee in the morning. The beauty of an evening sunset. The magic sound of laughter.
>
> This is the theme of Thornton Wilder's Pulitzer prize winning play, *Our Town*. It is also the message of Eastern philosophies that encourage adherents to "Be Here, Now." In other words, put the past behind you; plan and work for the future; but be here, *now*.
>
> Best Wishes, Mick
> Mick Zais, Ph.D.
> State Superintendent of Education

As our Ts suggest, you need to have the right Teachers, who willingly give of their Time to Train you. All of that Training is designed to help you reach your *there*. As important as all that is, you can miss the entire point of Transformation if you are not Thankful and appreciative, as Dr. Zais said, for your "*here* and *now.*" Until you find room in yourself to truly be Thankful for all you have been given, the next gift, lesson, or investment by your Teachers will be wasted, for the most part. You won't enjoy the process or the destination.

There are always nicer possessions you could buy, more elaborate vacations to take, or services you could purchase. But if you are not enjoying what you already have, what good is it? You must learn to be Thankful and enjoy your *here* as you move to your *there*. If not, when you get *there* you will be, in attitude and heart, what you were *here*. Byron Fields says, "A change of mind is better than a change of location." You can keep changing locations, but keep running into yourself as our Quaker friend so well states. Thankfulness will change that.

Thanksgiving Works like a Valve

If a valve in a line is shut, whatever is in that pipe remains. When the valve is opened, the contents flow in or out. Thanksgiving is a valve to your heart. When open, hate and bitterness can flow out and love and enthusiasm can flow in. While our Teachers Transmit themselves to us . . . make sure you are Thankful they are willing to Teach, and pray that they Transmit Thanksgiving.

A SIMPLE OBSERVATION:
Dr. Wayne Dyer says, "Happy people live in a happy world and angry people live in an angry world and the irony is, it's the same world."

THINGS TO THINK THROUGH:
- Who exemplifies a Thankful heart in your life?
- Have you Thanked them for their example?
- When you give Thanks, who do you give Thanks to?

- Have you seen your "environment" change when you worked with a Thankful spirit?
- What kind of people are you finding in your world?

ANCIENT WRITINGS: "In every thing give thanks, for this is the will of God in Christ Jesus concerning you."

BOOKS: *7 Laws of Highest Prosperity* by Cecil O. Kemp Jr.
The Generosity Factory by Ken Blanchard and S. Truett Cathy

MOVIE: *Treasures of the Snow*

I WILL APPLY THIS PRINCIPLE BY:_____

_____

_____

_____

It would be inappropriate for me to include Dr. Zais' words in a chapter on Thanksgiving, without saying, "Thank You, Dr. Zais."

I need a Teacher to help me move from here to there. When I have a Target, the proper Teacher will naturally Transmit the Terms and appropriate Technique(s) to me. When accompanied with Trust, this Training will influence my Thoughts and help me understand the Tools and Technology, along with the Tricks of the Trade. If the teacher lives Truth (or not) and allows Trips, it will help. Over Time the process will Transform me so I can Teach. If we continue to Trust and practice Thanksgiving, it will accelerate the transformation! I will start my *Toil* . . .

CHAPTER S

Toil

Alvin Nabors is a trusted friend. We met when Mr. Nabors was in his early 80s and I immediately started greeting him, "How is my favorite neighbor?" One night as we were talking, I decided to ask him about his life and background.

"What is your biggest regret, Mr. Nabors?"

"Not learning to read . . . not going to school. My aunt was in the fourth grade when I was in the first and we cut school— played hooky. I got in the second and quit. The desks were too small and it took me so long to get there. Gene, I can go somewhere and not know I'm there. I can't read the sign. If I've not been there before, I don't know I'm there now."

"Not being able to read has made life difficult for you," I observed.

"Gene, the night I turned sixteen I started working in the mill and stayed there the rest of my life. Being unable to read has been a challenge."

Geography and Success

To make a simple geographical observation, without action you are stuck right where you are. Without the right foundation of Terms and the other Ts, you will not know which way to go and might have to work very hard to progress past your current situation, like Mr. Nabors.

A Process to Learn How to Toil/Work

For years I have heard, "The best way to learn something is the five-step turnover."

1. Someone will do it (whatever the "it" is).
2. You will watch them do it.
3. You will help them do it.
4. You will do it and they will help you.
5. You will do it.

We are back to the basics. Where do you want to go? Who can naturally show you how to get there? But the question needs to be expanded: Who can show you how with the right attitude?

Toiling Can Be More Fun if the Mind Works Right First

When you see the word Toil (or work), what do you immediately think of? A pick and shovel? Exertion which would cause your muscles to ache? Or do you think about your mind?

In *100 Ways to Motivate Others*, authors Steve Chandler and Scott Richardson share several wonderful insights about work. Steve tells this story, which I will paraphrase.

At one of their seminars, a woman came to them complaining about her job. "This job is hell on earth. The fact that I show up for it is surprising to me. My job is a total nightmare."

"What part of your job is a nightmare?" they asked.

"My phone is constantly ringing. I have two bosses, both telling me what to do. I have an inbox stacked with papers. I go home from work stressed out . . ."

Steve responds, "Okay. Let's suppose we could introduce you to a woman from Nigeria. Her husband has been dead for two years. She has had to eat out of garbage cans to feed her family. You can Train her to do your job. Once she is Trained, we will offer her your job. Do you think you could persuade her that your job was a nightmare? Would she like trading jobs with you?"

"Oh, no. It would not be a nightmare for her. It would be the greatest blessing in the world for her. She would be thankful to have this job."

"Okay, is it a blessing or a nightmare? You can't have both." Steve explains to the complainer, "You can choose another job or you can choose another perception. You are free."

By your Thinking you make events and jobs blessings or curses. It takes Toil, work, and energy to *think* right, just like it takes the proper Tools to physically *work* right.

How do you change your perception towards the work and Toil you must do Today?

What do you see?

GODISNOWHERE

God Is Now Here helps the attitude more than God is No Where. Both options are in the line above. We can say, "We are stuck and there is not a chance we can get this fixed." Or, "We have a challenge. When we solve this one, we will make the history books." One makes winning *im*-possible, the other, possible. Either way, you choose. Confucius, Henry Ford, and a dozen others supposedly said, "The man who *says he can*, and the man who *says he cannot*, are both correct." Approach your work with the right mindset; it will change attitudes and outcomes.

Toil Is Required . . . Toil Spelled – WORK

Wanda Wilson, my good friend and encourager, went on a diet. Being the friends we are, I asked her about her progress.

Smiling, she said, "I joined a club that guarantees success. 'Join us—pay $29 a month—and lose weight.'"

"Have you lost any weight?"

"No," she responded immediately. "Taking the money to them every month does not take off the pounds. They expect me to *do* something."

As cosmetics company founder and CEO Estee Lauder put it: "I didn't get here by dreaming about it or thinking about it—I got here by doing it."

Get the Confusion Out

Where there is confusion, productivity stops. If you don't know where and why you are going somewhere or supposed to do something, progress stops. Clarity of the Target (Chapter B) is essential to progress in your chosen or assigned Toil. People who succeed usually LOVE what they do. Yes, there are days when it is hard, but the passion/love has to be there. When Magic Johnson became eligible for the college draft, the coach from Michigan State was at his house by daybreak. Johnson was not there. He had left, cleaned the snow off a community basketball court, and was practicing. Johnson is quoted: "Besides just loving the game, I had good coaches early—good size, good parents, everything I needed." But Johnson was clear on what he was out to do. He desired to be a pro. He loved the Toil/word required to get there. If you are confused about the objective, the Toil turns into a nightmare and the stress will dampen the love of the pursuit.

Get the Challenge and Excitement

When the love for the Task (either selected or assigned) is there, enthusiasm and passion flow. When your heart is fully engaged in the process, you will find the Time factor disappears. You will be working and discover that four hours have passed and you were not aware of a moment. Nothing great has ever happened without enthusiasm.

Rich DeVos (billionaire) was asked about his success. His comment was: "Every day I went to *work*." (Accent added.) Some people just go to work and forget to work once there. Mr. DeVos loved the process and engaged himself fully in it.

Chuck Coonradt (manager consultant), who wrote *The Game of Work,* was asked to find a solution for the poor performance of employees in a pre-constructed housing market. Steve Chandler tells the story on his audio series *100 Ways to Motivate Others.* The employees were described as people who moved as though they were arthritic snails in wet cement. But when they heard the lunch buzzer, enthusiasm and excitement jumped out of these same employees. They dropped their hammers as if they were shocked with 110 volts. They ran down the factory floor and played basketball at full force for forty-two minutes. Everyone knew their job and supported the team. At 12:42 the game stopped. They picked up their lunches and at 1:00 were back on the clock, moving slowly. Coonradt developed a process he calls, *The Motivation of Recreation*. By bringing the same motivational Tools to the work place they used in their game, morale shot up. Coonradt says those characteristics are *feedback, score-keeping, goal-setting, consistent coaching, and personal choice*. When these factors are in place, the self-employed entrepreneur and/or the employee is challenged to become his or her best.

An example of making this small mental switch can be seen when people complain if they have to work in a cooler or freezer at work. They don't have to come to work until eight AM, get breaks to warm up, but may complain anyway. The same people will get up at four AM and hike three miles through the snow in freezing weather to sit in a deer stand for hours. It is all in how you view the Toil you face Today.

Vince Lombardi is quoted to have said, "The only place success comes before work (Toil) is in the dictionary." Since work is an essential part of becoming what you desire to be, work with the right mindset.

Consider this poem by Edgar A. Guest

How Do You Tackle Your Work?

How do you tackle your work each day?
Are you scared of the job you find?
Do you grapple the task that comes your way
With a confident, easy mind?
Do you stand right up to the work ahead
Or fearfully pause to view it?
Do you start to toil with a sense of dread
Or feel that you're going to do it?

You can do as much as you think you can,
But you'll never accomplish more;
If you're afraid of yourself, young man,
There's little for you in store.

For failure comes from the inside first,
It's there if we only knew it,
And you can win, though you face the worst,
If you feel that you're going to do it.

Success! It's found in the soul of you,
And not in the realm of luck!
The world will furnish the work to do,
But you must provide the pluck.
You can do whatever you think you can,
It's all in the way you view it.
It's all in the start that you make, young man:
You must feel that you're going to do it.

How do you tackle your work each day?
With confidence clear, or dread?
What to yourself do you stop and say
When a new task lies ahead?
What is the thought that is in your mind?
Is fear ever running through it?
If so, just tackle the next you find
By thinking you're going to do it

A SIMPLE OBSERVATION:

What you write in the lines below, is more important than
what I wrote in the lines above. What you do with what you
write is more important than either.

THINGS TO THINK THROUGH:

- How do you view your work? Nightmare or fun?
- Who can Teach you to love your work?
- When will Wanda lose weight? When will you move on?
- Is Coonradt right? Can we get the *Motivation of Recreation* into
  our work lives and change our energy level?
- Since work does come before success, what are you going to do
  today to advance in the direction of your dream?

ANCIENT WRITINGS: "The LORD God took the man and put him in the Garden of Eden to work it and take care of it."

BOOK: *The Game of Work* by Chuck Coonradt

I WILL APPLY THIS PRINCIPLE BY:_____
_____
_____
_____

I need a Teacher to help me move from here to there. When I have a Target, the proper Teacher will naturally Transmit the Terms, and appropriate Technique(s) to me. When accompanied with Trust, this Training will influence my Thoughts and help me understand the Tools and Technology, along with the Tricks of the Trade. If the teacher lives Truth (or not) and allows Trips, it will help. Over Time the process will Transform me so I can Teach. If we continue to Trust and practice Thanksgiving, it will accelerate the transformation!

I will start my Toil—*Today* . . .

CHAPTER T

Today

If you ever get a chance to go camping with my wise friend Robby Dismukes, you might find him sharing this riddle with first-time campers.

The weather was changing. The Canadian geese woke up one brisk fall morning with cold feet. They could see their breath. The wise old goose said, "*Today* we are heading south." The entire flock packed their things. That is, all except one yearling. He liked it here and decided he would stay. He *knew* what he was doing.

The others tried to convince him more changes were coming, but he would not budge. So the flock took flight. They formed their V-formation, started quacking encouraging sounds to each other, and headed south.

After a few chilling mornings and second thoughts, the yearling decided he had made a mistake and headed south. He didn't have a V-formation or encouragement. Instead, he was working to get there—alone.

He had not flown far when icy blasts started pelting his head and wings. The rain began to freeze on his feathers, making them heavy, and he eventually crashed in a farmer's field.

He was lying in a half-frozen state when a compassionate cow approached. Seeing the young, immature goose freezing to death, she decided she had a couple of options. In a loving, motherly fashion, she pooped on the freezing goose to keep it warm.

The yearling didn't understand and began to mumble complaints in his half-frozen state.

The cow, sensing her care was not received warmly, decided the only other thing she could do was to wash the goose. So she backed up and peed on it.

The ice (along with the poop) slid off the urine-warmed goose and he continued to revive. Immediately, the ungrateful goose began to complain, curse, and show disrespect for his gracious benefactor—becoming even more profane than before.

A farmer, hearing the piercing noises, approached and found a healthy goose so engrossed in cursing the cow that he easily snatched it up and took him home.

The goose calmed down once he was inside the warm home. The farmer cleaned the goose with great care, for which the goose was appreciative. A few minutes later, the farmer cut off his head and cooked him for supper.

Robby will sit silently, waiting for a response.

"Is that it?" one of the kids will ask. "What a dumb story. I thought you were going to share something important."

Then Robby will pull out six, one-dollar bills. "There are six morals to this story. I will give you a dollar for each one you name."

The guessing starts . . .

I won't offer you a dollar, but you can either go to 21-Ts.com or e-mail your request to Info@21-Ts.com, and we will return the answers.

Here is one answer.

1. Today is the right Time to do the right thing. Don't procrastinate on important decisions and projects.
2.
3.
4.
5.
6.

What are you going to do Today about your Teachers? About the Targets you want to pursue? What about the Terms you need to learn and use? What part of the new Technique do you need to apply in a Tenacious fashion?

Something Important to Do Today

Everything starts with an idea or dream. We will never become more than our thinking will allow, so let's start stretching our brains—Today.

My favorite second son, Andrew, taught me a great lesson through his ability to dream big or select large and amazing Targets. He once had a T-shirt with an image imprinted on the front of a small boy who was maybe five years old. The boy stood with shoulder pads on, helmet under arm, staring into a football stadium the size of the Bank of America Stadium where the Panther's play in Charlotte, NC. Below the little fellow were these words: Dream Big.

When Andrew was four, I was working in Indianapolis, Indiana, and living in South Carolina, so my family and I traveled back and forth on a regular basis. During one of those trips, the entire family was sleeping, except Andrew and me.

Andrew broke the silence. "Dad, I wish it would rain diamonds and pearls."

"How come, Son?"

He paused for a second. "I would get every plastic bag in the house and I would go out in the yard and fill them up."

For once, I allowed him to think without interrupting.

"I would make my mama a dress," he said.

"Then I would make her some shoes, a bracelet, a ring, a necklace, and a hair bow." He paused again, collecting his thoughts. "And she would be beautiful."

There is a big dream inside every one of us. However, most of us never live our "diamonds and pearls dream" because we settle for so much less. Fear, guilt, and a thousand other things hold us back like a six-ton anchor attached to a twelve-foot john boat. That anchor keeps our little dream stuck in the mud of mediocrity. Seemingly, with little to no chance of dislodging the anchor and moving on, we stay right where we are.

Today is a great day—if you know how to live right here and right now. Otherwise, it is just another *there* with the same problems you allowed or built at your last *there*. To make Today the day you launch into a new ocean of opportunities, get a dream bigger than your fears and excuses.

If the principles of this book are ever going to work for you, you must cast off the anchor and set sail—Today—or you could end up in the farmer's pot.

Today's assignment is to begin writing what your ideal, perfect day would be like if you could see unseen lands through the eyes of faith (and an older goose), and start moving in that direction. I am going to ask you the same question I asked Daniel Ross: "What would you do with your life if time, contacts, and money were not an object?"

A SIMPLE OBSERVATION:
You can do (almost) anything, but you can't do everything.

THINGS TO THINK THROUGH:
- Who is the wiser, elder goose in your life? How well are you listening to his/her advice?
- Are you building respect for your elders and Teachers into the core of your Ts?
- Do you receive elders as gifts or curses?
- Do you complain and delay obedience after an elder speaks wisdom into your life?
- Are you like the yearling goose in any way?

ANCIENT WRITINGS: "Listen to my latest dream . . ."

BOOK: *Over the Top* by Zig Ziglar

I WILL APPLY THIS PRINCIPLE—TODAY—BY: Deciding what I would do with my life if Time, contacts, and money were not an object: _____
_____
_____

I need a Teacher, to help me move from here to there. When I have a Target, the proper Teacher will naturally Transmit the Terms, and appropriate Technique(s) to me. When accompanied with Trust, this Training will influence my Thoughts and help me understand the Tools and Technology, along with the Tricks of the Trade. If the teacher lives Truth (or not) and allows Trips, it will help. Over Time the process will Transform me so I can Teach. If we continue to Trust and practice Thanksgiving, it will accelerate the transformation! I will start my Toil—Today.

There will be many *Tests* . . .

CHAPTER U

Tests

Test 1: IS IT ALWAYS TEST TIME?

"Where are your tassels—the ones like your brother wore?" That was my mother's question as we walked from the car to one of the final events of my college career.

I responded, "Mom, John graduated magna cum laude. I am graduating thank the Lordy."

My family and I continued toward the hall. I sincerely thought I had arrived. I was *there,* leaving college. As we approached the door I was handed a brochure which read, "Commencement Exercises."

Wait a minute . . . this says "commence." I might have made the upper 95% of my graduating class possible, but I understand this word—commencement. It means to start, begin, origination, or something to do with being close to a starting point. Is this a trick? Should this brochure say "Completion Exercises" instead?

That day, an ever-so-small light came on in my thinking. Graduation was not about finishing, but starting.

Tests Are Part of Both Worlds

During our formal education, we had Tests at the end of sections and chapters on a regular basis and our teachers gave us pop Tests occasionally. We could always count on a Test. The funny thing is, I am still Tested daily, even though I've been out of college for decades.

I am in my mid-fifties and still *commencing*, constantly starting a brand new *here* when I think I am finished and finally *there*. I thought I would never see another Test after college, but in reality, they have quadrupled after my formal education ended. This book has been a major Test in my willingness to be Tenacious, working with a completely new set of Tools, Terms, and Teachers. You will find new opportunities every day that will become Tests of your resolve.

Many People Have Failed the Target Test

When I was building my sign business, I would often chat with a receptionist or tour a facility with a customer. I have always been curious about why and how a person chooses his or her line of work. So I conducted an informal survey to find out.

"Joe, how long have you worked *here*?" I would ask.

Answers varied from, "This is my first day" to "I have been here thirty-six years."

"Why did you decide to work *here*?"

Usually, the interviewee would take a few seconds to respond. The most common response was, "To be honest, I applied at *seven* places and this company offered me a job."

That seems like a weak reason to be employed for ten or more years with a company but, unfortunately, it was a common reason (or excuse).

My final question was usually an eye-opener: "Did you plan on staying *here* that long?" Almost always a simple, "No." tumbled from their lips.

Time after time I learned they had no real reason to start or stay. It was *not* a matter of planning, a Target, or excitement. My hosts knew they were not *where* they belonged.

After years of asking those questions, I only recall two men who gave me a convincing, "Yes, I planned on staying this long." One was a polished, polite, and professional black gentleman in Gaffney, SC. He told me that thirty-plus years ago he applied at Timken Bearing with a desire to make a career *there*. He respected the company and had given himself in exchange for a secure future. It worked for him. You could see it in the way he carried himself.

The other yes was from a short, stocky-built, white man at Diversified Machine in Pauline, SC. He, too, walked with confidence, gave himself wholeheartedly to the job, and was focused. He enjoyed working w*here* he was and with whom he was with.

Why do they stand out? Could it be they had set a Target, and were living their dreams? They apparently had evaluated life, their talents, and were pursuing their Target with the right Thoughts. They were content.

Why did you choose these Teachers, classes, or the Trade you are pursuing? Do you know?

As we have discussed, those choices are taking you somewhere and your choices will have consequences. If you do not like the path you are on—stop. Do not go through a Transition to be disappointed with the Transformation you experience at the end of the process.

Maybe you are heading in the direction of your parents' dream for you. Maybe a counselor or receptionist made a suggestion you followed. Are you pursuing *your* dream?

Why Many People Miss Their Dream

There are many factors involved in Transitioning to your *there*, as we have discussed, but what is pushing you from within? I often say, "More important than what you drive, is what drives you."

Dr. Kenneth Foutz, another one of my college professors often asked, "What keeps most people from their dream?" He would answer his own question with, "A new car." I am not kidding. He would say, "Many people graduate from college, start making some "real" money and think, I deserve a new car. They begin their after college years in debt and never free themselves of it." You will need to overcome many obstacles to reach your dream. Are you prepared to deny yourself those things which hold you back?

My wife says the only reason I am in the sign business is because "I was hiring." I love to dream, design, and develop creative solutions for my customers. But in my fifties, I know this is not my ultimate dream. Talking to you is my dream. I want to design and develop creative products that will help solve our greatest challenges—mentally and emotionally—so we can both reach our greatest dreams.

In answer to the third question I asked in my informal interview ("Did you plan on staying *here* that long?") I have to answer, "No," as did nearly all of my interviewees. I started a business to feed my family until I could get back to what I *really* wanted to do. When you are in your teens, you may see the future as a slow-moving train, but the speed changes quickly. People say "time flies." That is not true. As radio host Dr. James Dobson said on his daily radio program, "Time stays. We fly." I have flown. I have given twenty-plus years of my life to the sign business. Why? Was I unwilling to work through another Transformation as I am currently doing?

You are *here* but you are moving to *there* at the speed of light. Stop and deal honestly with your situation. Stephen Covey says, "The key is not to prioritize what is on the schedule, but to schedule your priorities." Are you?

THINGS TO THINK THROUGH AT Test #1
- ◆ Are you committed enough to your Target to say No to potential sidetracks, so you can do what you really love to do?

I WILL APPLY THIS PRINCIPLE BY WRITING my dream and what I desire my life to be like in five months and in five years.

_____

_____

_____

_____

Test 2: DEALING WITH CHALLENGES

How did you get here? I think you will find you got here by the Ts. Teachers, Terms, and Training came at you from 100 different directions and you were "Ah-Chooed" on. Naturally Transformation took place because of the Teachers who entered your life. You were infected. Some of what you "have" may be exactly what you want. Other "infections" you may wish you could get antibiotics for.

The Truth is: you can stay where you are with the same teachers and be infected with more of the same. Or a brand new case of "something" can be given to you, if you are willing to change Teachers.

Tests of Yesterday

I failed more Tests than I passed. School was not my thing. When two of my sons graduated from college with 99.543 and 99.542 averages (on the same day), they mentioned they both had only one B. When I graduated from college I could brag about the same thing: I only had one B too. Unfortunately, the rest of my grades were *below* B.

Life has also been filled with failure. I regret many of my actions. I looked at a lot of things I should have turned my head from. I stole so many items as a teenager I could have filled a warehouse with the goods. How stupid. There were days I just didn't think. I could have ended up like my friend I visit in jail. With all those failures in my past that I could not make right, I could have made, repeated failure my destiny.

Tests of Today

As I look at my current life, right *here* and right *now*, it is not perfect. This week I had a big struggle with my daughter. She is the most beautiful, wonderful girl in the world, but Briana and I found ourselves at odds with one another—in a mess. I responded poorly to her needs and totally dropped the ball.

When our current *here* has those types of challenges, there are only two things to do to keep the relationship right. Seek forgiveness and offer it. Then life again runs smoothly.

Tests of Tomorrow

As I look to the future, I know I can't pass all the Tests *there* either. Almost every religion teaches forgiveness along with the eternity doctrine I mentioned earlier. Every religion that I am aware of has a time when you will settle accounts with your Creator. Why is that? Do you believe there is something more? Do you realize you are fearfully and wonderfully made? Do you believe there might be a Higher Power?

When life does not turn out as planned and you are frustrated—what do you do? When you fail a grade? When you can't find work? When you believe you are supposed to be living a free and abundant life, but find yourself imprisoned by others and frustrated by your own bad choices— where do you look? Are you limited? Tangled? Trapped? How do you respond?

It Is a Matter of Faith

I believe the best way to respond is to recognize that you were created by Someone and then act accordingly. Our Declaration of Independence in the United States says, "We hold these truths to be self-evident, that all men are created equal, that they are endowed by their Creator with certain unalienable Rights; that among these are Life, Liberty, and the pursuit of Happiness." Note the wording—we are endowed by our Creator. Our response is a faith issue. I pass Tests by faith (past, present, and future). I always try to remember that the baby in the manger was Jesus. He was called Teacher often by His followers. I choose to embrace His teachings as my foundation (He is the Term). I choose to follow Him (Ah-choo). A perfect Teacher/example can be hard to find, so I searched until I found One I believed was worth following.

Jesus' life did not start with ideal circumstances. The government caused his family grief. He was not treated kindly or with respect. So what did He do? He overcame by the power of The Spirit within and looked forward to what lay ahead. Consider keeping your eye on Him.

A Great Eraser

Good Teachers have erasers. I believe Jesus is the Great Eraser. He takes all my messes, sins, and regrets—looks them over real good—and erases them. I do not need to let my shameful deeds keep me stuck in the past. Neither do you. I believe that, "God showed his great love for us by sending Christ to die for us while we were still sinners."

Shame keeps so many of us from moving to the next level. The fights of yesterday and the fears of tomorrow can crush the joy and fulfillment of Today. Let Him do what He does best. The author of this poem is unknown, but a John Wooden speech is where I heard it.

> At God's footstool, to confess,
> A poor soul knelt and bowed his head.
> "I failed," he cried. The master said,
> "Thou didst thy best. That is success.

The question is, what Teacher will we seek to show us how to make the *here* we are experiencing bearable and abundant?

You can take the past, present, and future Tests any way you want. But for my dollar, I am betting on Jesus. To be honest, I can't figure out God at all. I take life (and death) by faith. Just make sure you remember the barber. Don't give away too many dollars, thinking the kid is the idiot.

Building Your Habits

There is an old cliché which says habits begin as a thread so small you cannot see them, but become such strong cables that you cannot break them. Are you working on your habit to accomplish the most important tasks? Are your priorities being adjusted in your current *here* as you stretch towards your desired *there*?

We know that exercising thirty minutes a day will benefit us physically and emotionally. Knowledge is not the total key to the success of that statement. Doing it is. Discipline is the deciding factor.

THINGS TO THINK THROUGH AT Test 2 (along with repeating #1):

- ◆ Are you committed enough to your Target to say No to potential sidetracks, so you can do what you really love to do?
- ◆ Are you developing the disciplines to free yourself of unnecessary distractions (past, present and future) to make the Transition?

I WILL APPLY THIS PRINICIPLE BY: writing out the top six priorities for my actions Today and begin working on them by order of priority:

1) _____
2) _____
3) _____
4) _____
5) _____
6) _____

Test 3: PASSION AND PURPOSE

Tucker, my oldest son, and his teammates had studied. The mental preparation was tedious and extensive. They were preparing to compete against several other teams in an academic arena. It was going to be fast and furious. The first day of competition had arrived. Back and forth the contestants worked the buzzers and answered questions throughout the day. At the end of the event, the winning team was announced. Unfortunately, Tucker's team lost.

"We do have a high scorer award," the emcee announced. "For exceptional individual effort, we would like to recognize Tucker Burgess." Tucker went forward to receive his gold medal.

After the event, Tucker went to the event planners and asked if the same trophies would be given away at every competition. He then set a Target/goal to win the trophy at all three events. His Target became a passion.

The second round of competitions was scheduled. All the teams and individuals studied, prepared, and made ready for the event. The students hit the buzzers and, again, the competition was exciting. When the scores were tallied and the announcements made, Tucker's team lost, but he won the personal excellence trophy—again.

After the event, a "wormy" kid from Alabama approached Tucker and issued a challenge. "At the next event, I don't know if my team will win, but I am going to take that last gold medal." He wasn't rude; he was just stating his goal and desire.

There was trouble brewing . . .

Tucker came home and went to work. His team studied and they were ready. We traveled to Hendersonville, NC, for the final competition. Late that afternoon the testing came to an end. Our hearts raced as we waited for the results. Our team finally won a meet. Tucker and his teammates received their well-deserved trophies.

"Ladies and gentlemen, you have all waited for this moment. The high scorer today is . . . The "wormy" kid from Alabama." (Not the emcee's exact words—but close.)

Tucker stomped out of the room, around the corner, and into the bathroom. I followed him. "Son, get out there and congratulate that boy. Be a good winner."

Reluctantly, and because I outweighed him by 100 pounds, he exited the bathroom. I stood there staring in the mirror, wanting to cuss and kick the trash can. (I was not acting Response-Able.)

A few minutes later, a boy came into the bathroom and told me Tucker won. It took me a minute to understand that Tucker had won the high scorer trophy–again. As I entered the auditorium, I saw Tucker on stage. The judges were announcing someone had added incorrectly and Tucker was indeed the high scorer.

Then I saw something I shall never forget—two teenagers crying on stage as the trophy was taken from the "wormy" kid and given to Tucker. I learned something about competition that day. Many people play. Many people want to win, but very few make the game a passionate Target— something they are willing to work and study and even cry for. These two boys were the exception.

Different Strokes

Some people like golf. Some like track. Others enjoy softball, baseball, the arts, academics, military service, literature, or a hundred other things. I don't expect Tucker to cry if he loses in golf because golf is not his Target. But I do expect him to cry about *something*.

The television network ABC used to have a television program called "The Wide World of Sports." Their theme was: "The thrill of victory and the agony of defeat." Find your passion and pursue that dream. Sometimes you will have the thrill of victory and other times the agony of defeat. But get up and go for your Target again and again and again, until you reach it.

If you are having a difficult time finding your passion, ask yourself what causes you to get emotional, and maybe even cry when you think about it. Ask yourself what causes you to lose all sense of time as you pursue that Target? That, my friend, will help you uncover the passionate Targets you currently have.

Enjoy the Journey

In the *Cars* movie, the sexy little female car takes the sports car to the top of a curvy mountain road.

"Why don't people use this road any more?" the sports car asks. In the background you can see all the cars and trucks passing on the super highway in the valley.

"Years ago," she says, "people used to be concerned that they were having a great time. Now all they concern themselves with is making great time."

Hilton Johnson is one of my favorite coach and trainer personalities. He wrote, **"If you're not enjoying the journey, is the goal worth it?"** Which is more important to you, getting there or enjoying the journey?

Doing Your Best

This poem was written by a terminally ill young girl in a New York hospital. She had about six months to live. As her dying wish, she wanted to send a letter telling everyone to live their life to the fullest. She knew she would never make it to prom, graduate from high school, get married, or have a family of her own—but she knew the value of a day.

Slow Dance

Have you ever watched kids on a merry-go-round?
Or listened to the rain slapping on the ground?
Ever followed a butterfly's erratic flight?
Or gazed at the sun into the fading night?
You'd better slow down. Don't dance so fast.
Time is short. The music won't last.

Do you run through each day—on the fly?
When you ask "How are you?" Do you hear the reply?
When the day is done do you lie in your bed
With the next hundred chores running through your head?
You'd better slow down. Don't dance so fast.
Time is short. The music won't last.

Ever told your child, "We'll do it tomorrow?"
And in your haste, not see his sorrow?
Ever lost touch, let a good friendship die
Cause you never had time to call and say hi?
You'd better slow down. Don't dance so fast.
Time is short. The music won't last.

When you run so fast to get somewhere
You miss half the fun of getting there.
When you worry and hurry through your day,
It is like an unopened gift . . . thrown away.
Life is not a race. Do take it slower
Hear the music before the song is over.

THINGS TO THINK THROUGH AT Test 3 (+ repeating # 1 & # 2)
- ◆ Are you committed enough to your Target to say No to potential sidetracks, so you can do what you really love to do?
- ◆ Are you developing the disciplines to free yourself of unnecessary distractions (past, present and future) to make the Transition to your Target?
- ◆ Are you passionate, Thankful and enthusiastic about your life, here and now, as you prioritize your attitudes and actions as you move to your there?

Test 4: THE MOST IMPORTANT TEST

I like to start and end on the same page. I started this book with a short section of one man's life which is absolutely amazing—Dr. Benjamin Carson. I will end this book with him as well. He wrote on his website, "The most important thing to me is taking your God-given talents and developing them to the utmost so that you can be useful to your fellow man, period. And, what really motivates me right now, to be honest with you, is the opportunity to get other people to understand what's important in life—and it doesn't have a whole lot to do with the accumulation of wealth, titles, degrees, or power. Even though, interestingly enough, when you do develop your God-given talents and you become valuable, those things just seem to accumulate."

Albert Schweitzer said, "Success is not the key to happiness. Happiness is the key to success. If you *love* what you are doing, you will be successful."

Let's Apply These Words

My son Stephen went to look for a puppy. I told him he was welcome to *look* all he wanted but that he wasn't to bring a puppy home. He still had two more years of college, and I didn't think he needed a dog. Stephen obeys his father, for the most part, but not on this day.

He, or should I say *we*, have the cutest boxer east of the Mississippi. *We* have a great pet named Abby that our entire family sincerely enjoys. Katelyn, our daughter with Down syndrome, and Abby have some things in common. They both look at you with understanding eyes. They both get very excited. They both occasionally let their tongue protrude. Stephen thinks Abby may have Downs too.

The following parable is as old as the Jewish nation. I share it in "Burgessfied" fashion from the life of Abby, and her first day in our home. Enjoy.

Abby's Transformation

The Burgess yard has *always* been full of creatures (this part of the parable is true). We have had a lamb, a horse, cows, dogs, cats, a pheasant, and even a pig or two, maybe even seven. When Abby was just a puppy, new to the Burgess yard, a terrible conversation took place on her very first visit to the barn. Abby was sniffing around the yard, acting like a happy, friendly, loving boxer when she wandered near the barn. Our horse, Horace, wasn't all that thrilled with Abby's nosiness.

"Hey, you pup."

Abby looked up, clearly startled.

"Pup, I want you to know that I am the favorite animal on this farm," Horace said. "I am the only one that gets brushed regularly. I pull the carriage for the Burgesses. They love me more than all the other animals. But I don't think I will lose my position to you. You will provide nothing to this farm."

Before Abby could respond, our young Jersey cow, Hefty (short for Heifer), jumped into the fray. "Wait a minute, Horace. I am the VIP (very important pet) here. I provide Mrs. Burgess with milk. She makes cheese and gives her children cool milk for breakfast. Mr. Burgess loves the ice cream. Certainly you have no more importance than I. But I would agree with you on one thing; that pup can offer nothing."

Poor Abby began to feel the rejection and loss of energy. *Can I add anything to the farm? What can I give, compared to these animals? What am I doing here?*

Before her thoughts could go too far south, the lamb jumped in. "Horace, Hefty, you are both wrong. I am the favorite animal on this farm. Look at the clothesline. Every piece of clothing there came from me. I give the family wool, which they use to make clothes, which keeps them warm. How could you two be any more special than that?"

Before Horace or Hefty could respond, our lamb, Snoopy, delivered her two cents worth of discouragement. "You two are right about one thing. That new pup can add nothing to this farm." All the animals joined in the laughter.

Abby was crushed. She tried to leave the barn but before she could get out, our little yellow hen, Henrietta, jumped in with both feet. "I am ashamed of you three. Why don't you think about what I provide here? Every morning they enjoy fresh eggs. I am the beloved pet. But that dog, she will have no place here. I agree with all of you. She will certainly contribute nothing."

Abby, brokenhearted, separated herself from the other animals as fast as her little paws would carry her. But as she left, she heard something about how our cat, Kate, was the quickest creature, catching all the pesky mice. Abby certainly didn't stay to hear *the rest of the story*. She ran toward the house, tears streaming down her ugly face.

There on the back porch lay Gunter, Tucker's *old* golden retriever. Immediately, the *newest* animal to the yard began pouring out her heart to one of the *oldest* animals on the farm.

Gunter listened as Abby told how she had nothing to offer anyone on the farm. Gunter knew Abby just needed a Teacher who could Transmit a few Truths.

When Abby's sad tale became repetitive as she rehashed the awfulness story, Gunter spoke over Abby's sobs, "They are right. I have been on this farm for years. I provide no service to anyone either." Gunter, due to her age and wisdom, knew Abby couldn't understand the explanation. It was obvious Gunter was going to have to find a way to Transmit this Truth. Gunter could tell Abby was at least glad to have another pet that offered *nothing*. Abby continued to sob. Gunter knew her Terms would take a while for Abby to grasp and that her Transformation might take even longer.

"How have you been able to stay so long?" Abby asked through her tears. "Why do they keep you around if you provide no service?"

Gunter continued the Training. "Those other animals are right. You won't pull the buggy, give wool, or catch mice, but don't worry about what

200

you *can't* do. Don't cry about those things. Abby, you must use the abilities your Creator gave you. If you use them, you don't have to worry about giving milk."

Abby sat as still as a cat sneaking up on a bird.

At that instant, Gunter heard Tucker's truck coming up the driveway. Her ears perked up, her tail started wagging, and with a sparkle in her eye, she looked at Abby. Gunter knew the moment had arrived where a Transformation could possibly take place.

Gunter leaped off the porch, barking wildly. She wagged her tail and jumped in circles to meet Tucker. As Tucker opened the door, Gunter hopped inside to lick his face. Both Gunter and Tucker jumped out of the truck, playing, running and jumping. Tucker tried to get to the house, but couldn't. Gunter was ready to wrestle.

Tucker grabbed her and wrestled her to the ground, rubbing her belly and head. They were enjoying every moment.

Tucker said, "Gunter, you are my favorite animal on this farm. I love you. I wouldn't trade you for every cow in Texas."

Gunter and Tucker both heard a loud squeal as Abby leaped from the porch and bounced straight toward the love.

Abby caught it. She would now live it and Teach it. The Training had taken place in a setting where genuine love was Transmitted. Love will Transform. Ask Gunter, Abby, or . . . Tucker.

THINGS TO THINK THROUGH At Test 4 (+ #1, #2, & #3)

+ Are you committed enough to your Target to say No to potential sidetracks, so you can do what you really love to do?
+ Are you developing the disciplines to free yourself of unnecessary distractions (past, present and future) to make the transition to your Target?
+ Are you passionate, Thankful and enthusiastic about your life, here and now, as you prioritize your attitudes and actions as you move to your there?
+ Do you love yourself enough—to be what you were created to be? (And not worry about what Horace is doing?)

When you Thankfully take and pass these Tests daily, you will be well on your way to living a Transformed life. I hope your Training Time is filled with loving your Creator and yourself, along with everything and everyone involved in the Transformation process. Because if it is, you will be Transformed naturally, just like you learned to speak English (or Swahili). Pick a Target which ignites *your* passion. And pursue *your* Teachers with care; they will determine what language you speak.

From *here* or *there*, I am cheering for you.
I love you,

Gene C. Burgess

EPILOGUE

What Will You Do?

Kathy and I were in Knoxville Tennessee enjoying a supper cruise on the Tennessee River. It was a perfect evening—soft music, lots of food, stunning scenery, and a beautiful wife to share it with. As we launched, our seats faced the west bank of the river. We floated along watching manicured yards, pools, and gardens fill the horizon. These were million dollar homes, but nothing unusual went through my mind. It was a splendid evening.

As we approached the halfway point of our cruise, the boat made a U-turn. All of a sudden, I realized we had traveled several miles to a different community. Now that we were facing the east bank, the homes were small and many in need of repair. But instantly, I noticed another difference. There had not been a single person in those manicured yards or pools. That perfect evening found the owners away at their favorite restaurant or traveling in Europe (who knows).

But on the east side of the river, I saw a father with his six or seven-year-old son, sitting on a five-gallon bucket . . . fishing. Many children ran to the bank with smiles and enthusiastic waves. They sent us on our way—with joy.

Do *not* get me wrong. I am not complaining that people on the west side had money and could spend it as they pleased. But that evening I realized there were people with a lot less who were enjoying what they had a lot more.

You could say some people on the west bank had reached their *there*. Some people on the east bank may have too.

Be Yourself

Coach John Wooden said: "The definition I coined for success is: Peace of mind attained only through self satisfaction in knowing you made the effort to become the best of which you're capable. Now, we're all equal there. We're not all equal as far as intelligence is concerned. We're not equal as far as size. We're not all equal as far as appearance. We do not all have the same opportunities. We're not born in the same environments, but we're all absolutely equal in having the opportunity to make the most of what we have and not comparing or worrying about what others have. I coined that in 1934."

I Leave You with the Poem -- *Opportunity* by Berton Braley

With doubt and dismay you are smitten-
you think there's no chance for you, son?
Why the best books haven't been written
    the best race hasn't been run,
The best score hasn't been made yet,
    the best song hasn't been sung,
The best tune hasn't been played yet,
    Cheer up, for the world is young!

No chance? Why the world is just eager
    for things that you ought to create
Its store of true wealth is still meager
    its needs are incessant and great,
It yearns for more power and beauty

more laughter and love and romance,
More loyalty, labor and duty,
No chance—why there's nothing but chance!

For the best verse hasn't been rhymed yet,
The best house hasn't been planned,
The highest peak hasn't been climbed yet,
the mightiest rivers aren't spanned,
Don't worry and fret, faint hearted,
the chances have just begun,
For the best jobs haven't been started,
the best work hasn't been done.

Berton Braley

Writers turn Thoughts into ink. Readers turn ink into Thoughts. By Transforming those Thoughts into appropriate action, you are Transformed.

YOUR TRANSFORMATIONAL STORY

Our plan is to continue to turn *your* thoughts and stories
into more ink.

If you have a story of Transformation, we would like to read it.
In 1600 words or less, please forward your story to
Submissions@21-ts.com.
Please note if the story is for:
men, women, young adults, or teens.

We plan to produce four sequels to this book with 21 stories in each
book.

I hope your Transformation story makes the next book.

ACKNOWLEDGEMENTS

A percentage of the profits from this book will go to educational projects in Haiti.

Thank you to:

Edsel P. and Donna Marie Burgess (Dad and Mom)
Edward and JoAnn Tucker (Father-in-law and Mother-in-law)

John & Sally Thornburg (for their contribution to many lives)

Sherman Swofford, Dave Shinault and Sean Zwiernikowski
(for their suggestions which changed my life)

For their contribution to this project:

Terry Gilmer
Chuck Wallington
Linda Gilden
Dr. Richard Spencer
Jeff Burgess
Lee Warren
Andrea Merrell
Esther Mullinax
Rowena Kuo
Jeny Lyn B. Ruelo
Rick Hackel
Gayle Riley (who faithfully runs Burgess Enterprises)

And to the memory of

Johnny L. Cook and Teresa Wilson

A special thank you to:

Tucker, Andrew, Stephen, Briana, and Katelyn
I am proud of you and honored to be your Daddy-0.

And a special, special thank you to:

Kathy D. Burgess
You have gone to the "Jumping-Off Point" with me several times.

A few times we have flown and a few times we have crashed (Tripped)
miserably.

Thank you for letting me "jump" again, holding on to God
and this book!
Together we will see her fly!
Thank you for loving me.
I Love You!

Burg

ENDNOTES

Introduction
1. Nido Qubien - *Seven Choices for Success and Significance* – Quote taken from Simple Truths promotional E-mail.
2. Steve Harris – Taken from a promotional e-mail for an interview between Jack Canfield and Steve Harris.

Chapter A - Teacher
1. John Wooden, Poem – Sources of Insight website http://sourcesofinsight.com/lessons-learned-from-john-wooden.
2. Quote from Phil Driscoll. – From a concert I attended over twenty-five years ago.
3. John 3:2 TLB.

Chapter B - Target
1. Mary Kay Ash – www.forbes.com/sites/amyanderson/2013/03/14.
2. Tony Miller – Conference at Restoration Church 2013.
3. Dr. Seuss – www.DenverPost.com.
4. Arthur J. Hoist's poem – From an article I clipped over thirty years ago and placed in my Bible.
5. Gilbert Kaplan – www.unsolvedmysteries.com/usm463137.html?t=Quotes.
6. Earl Nightingale – www.brainyquote.com/quotes/authors/e/earl_nightingale.html.
7. Proverbs 29:18 NIV.

Chapter C - Transmit
1. Dr. Drury – Cadre Meetings in the 1980s.
2. Brendon Burchard. *The Millionaire Messenger* (Free Press, 2011), 11.
3. Gilbert K. Chesterton –www.brainyquote.com/quotes/quotes/g/gilbertkc104904.html.

Chapter D - Terms

1. Chinese Union Version John 3:16.
2. Mark Twain, freewebs.com/jromrell/apps/auth/signup.
3. Haitian stats – http://www.shannonlitton.com/KORE foundation Haiti: unicef.org/infobycountry/haiti_statistics.html #91 (http://www.cal.org/co/haiti/hlang.html).
4. Costa Rica statistic – http://www.ifitweremyhome.com/compare/CR/HT.
5. Napoleon Hill – ThinkExist.com.
6. Dr. Mike Zais quote – http://ed.sc.gov/agency/superintendent/vision/index.cfm.
7. Matthew 7:24-25 MSG.

Chapter E - Technique

1. Ben Carson quote - *www.realbencarson.com/*.
2. Oprah Winfrey – http://en.wikipedia.org/wiki/Oprah_Winfrey.
3. Oprah Winfrey quote – http://www.brainyquote.com/quotes/quotes/o/oprahwinfr133623.html.
4. Viktor Frankl – *Man's Search for Meaning.*
5. Philippians 4:11-12 NIV.

Chapter F - Trust

1. Wooden/Riley quote – *A Paragon Rising Above the Madness*; http://www.amazon.com/100-Ways-Motivate-Yourself-Forever/dp/1564147754 http://sportsillustrated.cnn.com/vault/article/magazine/MAG1018605/
2. Proverbs 3:5 NIV.

Chapter G - Training

1. Richard F. Abrahamson – *A Taste of Chicken Soup for the Teacher's Soul.*
2. Sherwood Lingenfelter and Marvin Mayers – *Ministering Cross-Culturally.*
3. Proverbs 22:6 MSG.

Chapter H – Thoughts

1. Bryan Tracy – http://www.brainyquote.com/quotes/keywords/thought.html#rOFyZEXdW076O35Z.99.
2. Jim Rohn – http://www.mccormickklessig.com/insnewsletters/VSA/2010/ffmay2010.pdf.
3. Bernard Baruch – http://www.quotationspage.com/quote/41608.html.
4. Hilton Johnson Biz Tip of the Day, Copyright Hilton Johnson Productions, Inc. All Rights Reserved. Duplication permitted only with copyright, content, and subscription details unaltered.
5. W. Woodworth – http://www.theartofhappiness.net/happiness-resources/article-about-happiness/rochman-sofan-happiness-articles/article_your_mind_is_a_garden.html.

6. Benjamin Disraeli – www.goodreads.com.
7. David Ring – As heard on a radio talk show.
8. Proverbs 23:7 NASB.

Chapter I – Tools
1. Rich DeVos – Penguin Group 375 Hudson St, NY NY, 1993, – page 9 of *Compassionate Capitalism*, Page 80 & 81.
2. Ecclesiastes 9:10 NIV.

Chapter J - Technology
1. David Mickey Evans – Obtained from Lee Warren, editor.
2. Louis C.K. – http://teamcoco.com/video/louis-ck-springsteen-cell-phone.
3. Todd Duncan, *Time Traps: Proven Strategies for Swamped Salespeople*, Nelson Books 2004.
4. Bill Gates – http://www.brainyquote.com/quotes/quotes/b/billgates390682.html.
5. Luke 12:15 NIV.

Chapter L – Trade
1. Ralph Waldo Emerson – www.goodreads.com/quotes.
2. Matthew 25:16 NIV.

Chapter M - Truth
1. John 14:6 NIV.
2. Acts 4: 10-12 MSG.

Chapter N - Trips
1. Dr. Tom Orent – Thu 1/10/2013 4:38 PM (GKIC) Dave Dee [info@ dankennedy.com] (Tue 11/13/2012 12:36 PM A tip from GKIC's Platinum Mastermind to move your business forward before 2013).
2. Bill Cosby – https://www.goodreads.com/quotes/108613-in-order-to-succeed-your-desire-for-success-should-be.
3. John Maxwell – http://www.amazon.com/Failing-Forward-Turning-Mistakes-Stepping/dp/0785288570.
4. *Famous Failures* by Joey Green – http://www.amazon.com/Famous-Failures-Hundreds-Achieving-Phenomenal/dp/0977259021.
5. Charles C. Manz – Berrett-Keohler Publishers, Inc, San Franscisco.
6. Poem by Edgar Guest – http://www.poetryfoundation.org/poem/173583.
7. 3M – Wikipedia.
8. Fred Smith – Wikipedia.
9. Oprah Winfrey – https://www.goodreads.com/quotes/250874-i-don-t-believe-in-failure-it-s-not-failure-if-you.
10. Og Mandino – *The Greatest Salesman in the World,* http://www.quotationspage.

com/quote/38199.html.

11. Albert Einstein – http://www.brainyquote.com/quotes/quotes/a/
    alberteins109012.html.
12. Walter Disney – www.biography.com.
13. John Grisham – *en.wikipedia.org/wiki/John_Grisham.*
14. Akio Morita – *en.wikipedia.org/wiki/Akio_Morita.*
15. Michael Jordan – http://www.brainyquote.com/quotes/quotes/m/
    michaeljor167379.html.
16. Robert Townsend – *en.wikipedia.org/wiki/Robert_Townsend.*
17. Hilton Johnson – CoachTrainer® Biz Tip of the Day Thu 5/9/2013 6:55 AM.
18. Proverbs 24:15 TLB.

Chapter O - Time
1. Leo-Tzu – http://www.quotationspage.com/quote/39468.html.
2. Dr. Les Parrott – Recalled from an old story.
3. Old African proverb –Taken from the preface to the second edition of Lois J.
   Zachary's book, *The Mentor's Guide: Facilitating Effective Learning Relationships,*
   second edition.
4. Ecclesiastes 3:1-8 NIV.

Chapter P – Transformation
1. Albert Einstein – http://www.awakin.org/read/view.php?tid.
2. Luke 8:15 NIV.

Chapter Q – Teach
1. Charles Coonradt – *The Game of Work*, from introduction Gibbs Smith,
   publishing, 2001, Coach John Wooden.
2. Doctor James – James 3:1-8 MSG.
3. John Maxwell – *Success 101* © 2008, Thomas Nelson.
4. Og Mandino – http://www.brainyquote.com/quotes/quotes/o/
   ogmandino134856.html.
5. 2 Timothy 2:2 MSG.

Chapter R – Thanksgiving
1. Marcus Tullius Cicero – http://www.quotationspage.com/quote/2035.html.
2. Dr. Charles Swindoll – https://www.goodreads.com/quotes/267482-the-
   longer-i-live-the-more-i-realize-the-impact.
3. Willie Nelson – P 89 Simple Truths *Learning to Dance in the Rain…* The
   Power of Gratitude, Mac Anderson and BJ Gallagher.
4. Meister Eckhart – http://manyvoices.soundstrue.com/if-the-only-prayer-you-
   ever-say-in-your-whole-life-is-thank-you-that-would-suffice/#.Ul_2ZFP4IkQ.
5. Quote about shoes/feet – http://sonnysideuppp.blogspot.com/2010/04/i-had-

blues-because-i-had-no-shoes.html.

6. Dr Wayne Dyer – Tape series, *The Course of Winning*, Dennis Waitley Nightingale Conant 1989.

7. I Thessalonians 5:18 MSG.

Chapter S - Toil

1. *100 ways to Motivate Others*, narrators Steve Chandler and Scott Richardson CD # 3 and track 39 titled, Debate Yourself.

2. Estee Lauder – http://boardofwisdom.com/togo/Quotes/ ShowQuote?msgid=568413#.Ul_5WVP4IkQ.

3. Magic Johnson; http://www.answers.com/topic/magic-johnson.

4. Rich DeVos – Heard in an interview.

5. Chuck Coonradt – Page 180, *100 ways to Motivate Others*, CD narrators Steve Chandler and Scott Richardson.

6. Vince Lombardi – http://www.brainyquote.com/quotes/quotes/v/ vincelomba109282.html.

7. Edgar A. Guest Poem –http://www.happypublishing.com/spiritualthoughts/ how-do-you-tackle-your-work.htm.

8. Genesis 2:15 NIV

Chapter T - Today

1. Genesis 37:9 TLB.

Chapter U – Tests

1. Romans 5:8 TLB.

2. Stephen Covey – http://www.brainyquote.com/quotes/quotes/s/ stephencov133504.html.

3. Hilton Johnson – Thu 1/17/2013 8:41 AM Biz tip of the day.

4. SLOW DANCE – Dr. Dennis Shields, Professor, Department of Developmental and Molecular Biology Albert Einstein College of Medicine.

5. Ben Carson –http://www.mygrowthplan.org/Biographies/BenjaminCarson. html On What's Really Important In Life.

6. Albert Schweitzer (1875-1965) http://godspeoplesing.org/walls/Gifted_Hands. pdf.

7. Coach John Wooden –http://www.alastairhumphreys.com/selfsatisfaction- knowing-effort-capable/.

8. Berton Braley – http://www.everyday-wisdom.com/daily-inspiration- Oct-21-2008.html.

I need a Teacher, to help me move from here to there. When I have a Target, the proper Teacher will naturally Transmit the Terms, and appropriate Technique(s) to me. When accompanied with Trust, this Training will influence my Thoughts and help me understand the Tools and Technology, along with the Tricks of the Trade. If the teacher lives Truth (or not) and allows Trips, it will help. Over Time the process will Transform me so I can Teach. If we continue to⁻ Trust and practice Thanksgiving, it will accelerate the transformation! I will start my Toil—Today.

There will be many Tests . . .

Made in the USA
Charleston, SC
14 December 2013